De Gaulle

The World Generals Series

"Palgrave's World Generals Series features great leaders whose reputations have transcended their own nations, whose bold characters led to new forms of combat, whose determination and courage gave shape to new dynasties and civilizations—men whose creativity and courage inspired multitudes. Beginning with illustrious World War II German Field Marshal Erwin Rommel, known as the Desert Fox, the series sheds new light on famous warrior-leaders such as Giap, Alexander, Julius Caesar, and Lafayette, drawing out the many important leadership lessons that are still relevant to our lives today."

—*General Wesley K. Clark (Ret.)*

This distinguished new series features the lives of eminent military leaders from around the world who changed history. Top military historians are writing concise but comprehensive biographies including the personal lives, battles, strategies, and legacies of these great generals, with the aim to provide background and insight into contemporary armies and wars, as well as to draw lessons for the leaders of today.

Rommel by Charles Messenger

Alexander the Great by Bill Yenne

Montgomery by Trevor Royle

Lafayette by Marc Leepson

Ataturk by Austin Bay

De Gaulle by Michael E. Haskew

Julius Caesar by Bill Yenne

Giap by James Warren

De Gaulle

Lessons in Leadership from
the Defiant General

Michael E. Haskew

palgrave
macmillan

DE GAULLE
Copyright © Michael E. Haskew, 2011.

All rights reserved.

First published in 2011 by
PALGRAVE MACMILLAN®
in the United States—a division of St. Martin's Press LLC,
175 Fifth Avenue, New York, NY 10010.

Where this book is distributed in the United Kingdom, Europe, and the rest
of the world, this is by Palgrave Macmillan, a division of Macmillan Publishers
Limited, registered in England, company number 785998, of Houndmills,
Basingstoke, Hampshire RG21 6XS.

Palgrave Macmillan is the global academic imprint of the above companies
and has companies and representatives throughout the world.

Palgrave® and Macmillan® are registered trademarks in the United States,
the United Kingdom, Europe and other countries.

ISBN: 978–0–230–11081–6

Library of Congress Cataloging-in-Publication Data

Haskew, Michael E.
    De Gaulle : lessons in leadership from the defiant general /
Michael E. Haskew ; foreword by Wesley K. Clark.
        p. cm.—(World generals)
    Includes index.
    ISBN 978–0–230–11081–6
    1. Gaulle, Charles de, 1890–1970. 2. Gaulle, Charles de,
1890–1970—Political and social views. 3. Gaulle, Charles de,
1890–1970—Military leadership. 4. Political leadership—France—
History—20th century. 5. Presidents—France—Biography.
6. Generals—France—Biography. 7. France. Armée—Biography.
8. France—History—German occupation, 1940–1945. 9. World War,
1939–1945—Underground movements—France. 10. France—Politics
and government—1945– I. Title.

DC420.H37 2011
944.083′6092—dc22
[B]   2011014514

A catalogue record of the book is available from the British Library.

Design by Newgen Imaging Systems (P) Ltd., Chennai, India.

First edition: October 2011

10 9 8 7 6 5 4 3 2 1

Printed in the United States of America.

Contents

*Eight pages of black-and-white photographs appear
between pages 90 and 91.*

Foreword

No MODERN MILITARY COMMANDER HAS BEEN SO DISPARAGED IN British and US government, military, and media circles as Charles de Gaulle. Derided as arrogant, pompous, disdainful, and uncooperative, de Gaulle has been the butt of criticism in the West for 60 years. He was selfish, and difficult for Eisenhower and Churchill to deal with in World War II, threw NATO out of France in the mid-sixties, and seemed to go out of his way—as perceived by many Americans—to tweak America at every opportunity.

But this is a wholly one-sided impression. The truth is different. De Gaulle was in fact a great leader who played *the* critical role in shaping modern France. He is worthy of study, respect, and admiration. Michael Haskew's superb biography of this great French general and president brings de Gaulle and his great contributions to life; and more, it provides the context in which his achievements may be more accurately appraised.

De Gaulle was born in a middle class, conservative Catholic family. His father was an educator; an uncle was a notable political writer. The family had a history of military service dating back several hundred years. From his earliest years he was temperamental, strong-willed, and apparently infused with an overpowering sense of destiny—perhaps not surprising in one who grew up under the overhang of French defeat, rising German power, and an expectation of future conflict. But he also showed a keen sense for nuanced communication, for stratagy, and diplomacy, even in early writings.

He entered the military at 19. He was "trouble" from the beginning—argumentative, stubborn, self-righteous. His military schooling showed a good mind but also a truly remarkable sense of purpose. He wasn't one of the "good ol' boys." He carried these attitudes into his first assignments in the years prior to World War I, arguing for his insights and perspectives against officers far senior in rank.

He was a superbly dedicated junior officer, deeply concerned about his men, knowledgeable about their backgrounds, and thoughtful in the study of tactics and the implications of technology. And he brought a larger-than-life sense of honor and grandeur—even to his platoon of less than three dozen soldiers. Simply put, he was a standout, though by no means popular, junior officer.

On the battlefield he was incredibly brave. He was wounded and evacuated once, and he was wounded, left for dead, and captured a second time in the ferocious fighting around Verdun. He then tried numerous times, unsuccessfully, to escape—two years of struggles, until the war ended.

Perhaps there were some better combat records in the French Army, but, to be fair, his combat experience far exceeded his American contemporaries Generals Eisenhower and Bradley, and arguably George Patton as well. He had faced fire, led men, expected death, and proved himself tough, resourceful, courageous, and inspiring.

The French Army somehow found a place for him, even after two years of captivity, in its postwar ranks. But de Gaulle, now in his thirties, was intellectually precocious, impatient, and impervious to caution. Still a relatively junior officer, he wrote, lectured, and fought it out intellectually and philosophically with some of the top officers in the French military. His ideas on armored warfare were insightful and ran completely against the grain of the French defensive mindset and great investment in the Maginot Line. But his ideas on leadership focused on the "great man" theory: standing apart from the crowd, alone and unappreciated, but ready in a moment of crisis. How could it have been perceived as anything but self-serving? And, in fact, he was single-minded and intense in pursuit of recognition, advancement, and greater responsibilities. Not surprisingly, he earned the enmity of most of the top command and his contemporaries. He was headed nowhere until France mobilized for World War II.

Then, with the evidence of the Polish campaign, the French high command began to try to rethink its strategy and philosophy. De Gaulle was there and on the eve of the German attack into France in May 1940, and received command of the French Fourth Armored Division. Under fire, he formed it and struck, reformed it, maneuvered, and struck again into the flank of the German blitzkrieg. It was, of course, too little, and uncoordinated with higher command. But it was a tactical success and showed heroic senior-officer leadership, every bit the equal of a Patton or Rommel. In the dying days of the government his heroics captured the attention of the outgoing French prime minister and he was appointed undersecretary of state for defense, leapfrogging in authority over the entire French military chain of command. They were defeated and defeatist—de Gaulle, true to form, wasn't.

In the chaos of defeat and imminent surrender, de Gaulle formed a relationship with Churchill and the British, and rather than serve under a defeated government soon to be a German puppet, he fled for London and proclaimed himself the leader of the Free French.

It was a breathtaking step. In a month he had gone from armored division command to government minister to self-appointed head of government. Yet, he had nothing. No staff, no army, no money, and no country.

Perhaps this is the most compelling part of the story. Over the next four years he assembled the wreckage of France, picking and maneuvering his way forward, to the annoyance of the Americans Brits, and other French, who simply wanted a compliant partner and couldn't quite understand that this man, de Gaulle, was himself France. Four years of infighting later, he and his Free French marched triumphantly back into France, with de Gaulle as its rightful leader.

But, to his everlasting credit, de Gaulle worked to re-create French democracy. In the postwar voting, he was rejected. He withdrew, coming back a few years later with a parliamentary effort, lost ground, and then, as France sunk into near civil war amidst the conflict in Algeria he emerged, this time to create a new government with strong presidential powers. And then, he served as its president. He ended the colonial occupation of Algeria, put down a military revolt, created an independent French nuclear deterrent, and withdrew France from NATO's integrated command structure. He changed 80 years of troubled French democracy and gave France new stature and influence.

The story of modern France is the story of de Gaulle. Proud and arrogant, a "loner" with a huge ego—sure. But in the pantheon of modern history's military leaders de Gaulle is unquestionably one of the greatest: a courageous warrior, a visionary leader, and a man who reshaped his country. Haskew's sparkling, fast-paced biography makes great reading, in Europe and among military students everywhere. But it also should be read by every American interested in understanding Europe—and America.

—General Wesley K. Clark (Ret.)

Prologue

THE PHONY WAR WAS OVER. SUDDENLY AND VIOLENTLY, MONTHS of uneasy quiet had been shattered. Spearheads of German tanks and mechanized infantry knifed deeply into France and the Low Countries while Luftwaffe dive bombers pounded enemy positions and fighters swept the skies of Allied aircraft. Blitzkrieg had come to the West.

"They will open the road to great victories...their swift and profound effects will cause the enemy to collapse, as sometimes the breaking of a pillar can bring down a cathedral,"[1] one visionary had written of the prospects for rapid victory with the mailed fist of tanks and armored vehicles exploiting breaches in enemy lines to spread chaos, death, and destruction in rear areas.

The irony of the moment was not lost on Charles André Joseph Marie de Gaulle, the French army officer who had penned these words nearly a decade earlier. In his book *Vers l'Armée de Métier,* translated as *Towards a Professional Army* and later published in English as *The Army of the Future,* de Gaulle had seen the potential of mechanized warfare and advocated an army of 100,000 highly trained soldiers utilizing fire and maneuver to gain ground, demoralize an enemy, and degrade its ability to resist. On May 10, 1940, however, it was France that had been sent reeling by the devastating German onslaught early in World War II.

Always outspoken and assertive to the point of self-aggrandizement, de Gaulle had previously argued for an immediate expansion of the French capacity to field powerful armored divisions. His sense of urgency, however, was far greater than that of an interwar French military establishment caught in the economic vise of the Great Depression and haunted by the specter of World War I and its tremendous carnage. Much as his contemporary General J. F. C. Fuller had been quietly retired from the British Army for similar views, this previously obscure lieutenant colonel had been dismissed by senior French officers as an eccentric at best and a crackpot at worst.

The day after the German blitzkrieg commenced, de Gaulle was given command of the French 4th Armored Division, a unit that existed as much on paper as it did in men and machines. Within a week, those tanks and soldiers the commander could muster were thrown into the path of the German vanguard that had swept across the French frontier.

"Why not, even now, mass all our armor in one strike force and smash the Nazis to pieces?" de Gaulle demanded at Montcornet.[2]

General Alphonse Georges, a member of the staff of overall commander General Maurice Gamelin, replied, "The 1st Division was annihilated in Belgium. The 2nd Division was destroyed while in transport on the River Oise. The 3rd Division fought gloriously in bits and pieces but was overwhelmed. Yours is all that is left. There it is, de Gaulle. You have long held the idea that the enemy is putting into practice. Now is your chance to act!"[3]

Woefully under strength, the 4th Armored Division, with the striking figure of de Gaulle protruding from the turret of the leading tank, advanced to confront the German 10th Panzer Division. Resolute and utterly fearless on the battlefield, de Gaulle demonstrated the qualities of a commander under fire that would also serve him well later as a political figure and de facto leader of the French nation.

De Gaulle was determined to strike a blow against the invaders— for French pride if nothing else, and perhaps win a victory, Pyrrhic though it might be. With 200 tanks, he advanced and overran numerous German antitank gun positions. However, without artillery support and subjected to heavy air attack the counterthrust was eventually beaten back.

Two weeks later, de Gaulle fought the Germans again. Promoted to brigadier general, he was ordered to the River Somme, more than 120 miles away. The 4th Armored Division attacked a German bridgehead near Abbeville, captured more than 400 prisoners, and compelled the enemy to cross the Somme farther north. Greatly outnumbered, the French were unable to follow up their victory. Nevertheless, de Gaulle was credited with leading French forces against long odds and gaining one of the few military triumphs of the forlorn spring of 1940.

In early June, Prime Minister Paul Reynaud called de Gaulle to Paris. Although the Third Republic had only weeks to live, he appointed de Gaulle undersecretary of state for national defense and war. With the German Army advancing on all fronts, the fate of France was sealed. The Reynaud government resigned, and a collaborationist regime at Vichy, under the elderly Marshal Philippe Pétain, succumbed to a humiliating armistice that was signed on June 22.

A defiant de Gaulle had already departed France aboard an aircraft bound for Britain. Declared a traitor by the Vichy government, he was later sentenced to death in absentia. Before the Battle of France had officially ended, de Gaulle filled a substantial power vacuum and claimed the mantle of leader of the Free French. Addressing his people via BBC radio on June 18, he intoned, "France has lost a battle, but France has not lost the war.... Whatever happens, the flame of the French resistance must not be extinguished and will not be extinguished. Tomorrow, as today, I will speak on the radio from London."

As a leader, General Charles de Gaulle demonstrated tactical vision, personal courage, patriotism, and a sense of honor that stirred the pride of the French people during the darkest hour of their nation's history. While he was not always admired, his extraordinary drive, determination, and sense of purpose certainly command respect.

CHAPTER 1

Child of Flanders

From his earliest recollection to his dying day, Charles André Joseph Marie de Gaulle believed himself to be a man of destiny, and that destiny was—without question—intertwined with the past, present, and future of France. He was born on November 22, 1890 in the ancient city of Lille, a center of manufacturing and textile production in French Flanders near the border with Belgium.

He was the third child of Henri and Jeanne Marie de Gaulle, and the family was devoutly Catholic. Just a year before his birth, engineer Gustave Eiffel had completed has famous tower, which welcomed people to the 1889 Exposition Universelle in Paris. Although Charles had been born during the "Belle Epoque" (Beautiful Period), a period of tremendous flowering of art, literature, music, and philosophy, an undercurrent of shame resulting from a humiliating defeat in the Franco-Prussian War two decades earlier roiled within the sub-conscious of the French people.

The Prussian armies of Kaiser Wilhelm I and Chancellor Otto von Bismarck had dictated the terms of the surrender and the Treaty of Frankfurt in 1871, and the blow to French prestige had been severe. A veteran of that war who had been wounded during the siege of Paris, Henri de Gaulle longed for the day when the humiliating defeat of France would be put right and the amputated provinces of Alsace and Lorraine returned to the French fold. In addition to establishing German sovereignty in the two disputed provinces, the treaty had required their residents to declare French allegiance and vacate the territory or remain there and become German citizens. It further compelled the French government to recognize Wilhelm I of Prussia as emperor of the unified Germany, stipulated that France pay a war indemnity of 5 billion francs, and provided for the German military occupation of some French territory until the indemnity was paid.

Science and technology flourished during the Belle Epoque, and the period was defined by political stability among the nations of Europe as disputes were often settled through diplomatic means rather than armed conflict. Nevertheless, a rigorous class distinction had emerged, nationalistic rivalry and a burgeoning arms race threatened a lasting peace, and robust imperialism all but guaranteed that the great powers would challenge one another around the globe during the years to come. By 1914, old Europe would cease to exist. As Charles de Gaulle entered the world, the continent was at a crossroads.

Young Charles was often headstrong and petulant, teasing and annoying his brothers and sisters, acknowledging the authority of his father as necessary, but ignoring the direction of his mother. He was sometimes prone to tantrums, flailing his arms and crying loudly when he did not get his way. When the children played games, Charles exerted a force of personality such that even older boys took notice and followed his lead. Charles delighted in rounding up those who lived nearby and dividing them for competition, always assuming a principal role.

Even as a child, the majesty and splendor of a culturally preeminent France were never far from the mind of Charles de Gaulle. Once, with toy soldiers arrayed across the floor, his brother, Xavier, had declared his wish to be king of France rather than emperor of Germany. Charles retorted, "Never! France is mine." On another occasion, his younger brother, Pierre, cried out that Charles had hit him. The response had seemed quite appropriate to Charles when Pierre, whose role was that of a spy during a military game, had turned over a secret message to the enemy rather than devouring it.[1]

Although he sometimes tried the patience of his parents and siblings, the bonds of family and true affection among them were genuine and lasting, and Charles remained close to his mother and father throughout their lives. While Xavier rose to the office of consul general in Geneva, Switzerland, Pierre accompanied Charles during the turbulent years of World War II and later served in several government offices. Another brother, Jacques, may well have been the favorite of Charles, but a promising career in engineering was cut short by severe illness that left Jacques paralyzed and unable to speak. An older sister, Marie-Agnes, joined the Resistance during World War II. She was imprisoned by the Nazis and liberated by Allied troops in 1945, penned a personal memoir, and lived into the 1980s.

Despite his intense self-will, Charles's parents were influential in one aspect of the child's life above all. They instilled in him a reverence for his Catholic faith and a passion for his native country, immersing the boy in stories of the history of the French nation. Indeed, the de Gaulle family name had been associated with epic battles of the past, most notably Agincourt in 1415. Prior to that, a French nobleman named de Gaulle was said to have repulsed an English army that had invaded the country. Perhaps, then, it is not surprising that Charles de Gaulle would decide to pursue a career in the military, his self-will notwithstanding.

"My father," Charles wrote, "was a thoughtful, cultivated, traditional man, imbued with a feeling of the dignity of France. He made me aware of her history. My mother had an uncompromising passion for her country, equal to her religious piety."[2]

Another profound influence on the young man was his namesake, an elder Charles de Gaulle who was his uncle. The author of a book, *The Celts in the XIXth Century,* he had proposed the union of the Welsh, Scots, Irish, and Breton peoples. The uncle had also penned a pamphlet titled *The Awakening of the Race.* A passage from the short work stirred the martial and nationalistic fervor in young Charles. "In a camp, surprised by an enemy attack under cover of night," it read, "where each man is fighting alone, in dark confusion, no one asks for the grade or rank of the man who lifts up the standard and makes the first call to rally for resistance."[3]

Henri de Gaulle was an educator, and around the turn of the century he received an appointment as headmaster of the Jesuit College of the Immaculate Conception in Paris, moving the family to the capital city. When the French government enforced a separation of church and state in the country and closed the Jesuit schools, Henri founded his own modest school on the Rue de Postes and remained in Paris. Afternoons and weekends were spent at the tomb of Napoleon in L'Hotel des Invalides or admiring the Arc de Triomphe. There were also stimulating conversations around the dinner table, with his father and mother always teaching, questioning, and inviting the children to debate. Disagreements were often analyzed, distilled to their basic components, and then resolved as the result of thoughtful exercise.

Charles followed the path of Catholic education, receiving formal instruction from the Christian Brothers, the Jesuits at schools in Paris and then later at the College du Sacré-Coeur in Antoing, Belgium, and the College Stanislas in Paris. His early academic career was unremarkable. However, he loved philosophy, history, and literature, relying on a towering intellect and an exceptional memory to maintain an overall standing that was better than average. Such performance may be attributed to his continuing sense of superiority to both peers and instructors, while his prodigious memory allowed for passing grades in subjects of less interest to him. His affinity for the history of France led to his deep study of the nation's military past. He committed to memory the actions that occurred during most, if not all, of the country's great battles, including the strategic implications of the battles, troop movements, and individual unit orders.

Introduced to the Classics at an early age, Charles was familiar with Socrates and Plato. He explored the philosophical realm, and tried his hand at creative writing. When he was 14 years old, he penned a rhyming one-act play titled *Une Mauvaise Rencontre,* or *A Bad Encounter.* The writer describes the misfortune of a traveler who is accosted by a highwayman disguised as an unfortunate vagrant who proceeds to appropriate various articles of clothing from the wary victim, including his hat, shoes, and money bag, through a discourse in which the traveler is made to assume in the beginning that he is being generous. However, the vignette takes a pronounced turn.

The highwayman pleads, "Won't you save a soul before it is seized with the blind desire to kill a fellow man?" When the traveler hesitates, the highwayman offers one more compelling reason to comply. "Look here," he says, "I have two pistols cocked!"[4]

The young man's wit shines through in the short production, while also presenting a glimpse of that pragmatic perspective that guided Charles de Gaulle throughout his life. De Gaulle, a calculating and astute soldier and statesman, was never to be taken at face value. When the highwayman implores his victim to relent, the exchange reveals a tactic he later employed in dealing with heads of state, effectively urging them to accede to his demands. Otherwise, he would be forced to take some action that would be distasteful to all concerned.

The family enjoyed the morality play very much, and shortly thereafter someone forwarded the manuscript to a literary competition, where it was judged worthy of a prize. Charles was required to choose between having his work published or receiving a cash prize of 25 francs. De Gaulle chose to have the story appear in print, a more lasting reward than the fleeting gratification of a small sum of money.

Perhaps a more telling illustration of the vision that began to manifest itself in the youthful Charles was a work of fiction which he conceived the following year while attending the College of the Immaculate Conception in Paris. Conjuring up images of a future Europe embroiled in war, the 15-year-old wrote:

> In 1930 Europe, angered by the government's ill will and insolence, declared war on France. Three German armies crossed the Vosges. The command of the strongest army was entrusted to General von Manteuffel. The Field Marshal Prince Frederick Charles took the head of the second. In France everything was very rapidly organized.
>
> General de Gaulle was placed at the head of 200,000 men and 518 guns; General de Boisdeffre commanded an army of 150,000 men and 510 guns. On 10 February the armies took the field. De Gaulle quickly fixed upon his plan: he was first to save Nancy, then join hands with Boisdeffre and crush the Germans before they could unite, which would certainly have been disastrous for us.[5]

Somewhat prophetic, already visionary, the young man had captured the essence of the first 50 years of twentieth-century Europe—wars and rumors of wars. De Gaulle had traveled extensively in Germany and wrote that Europe was in the midst of sweeping change. He sensed a tide of unrest and even hostility toward his country and noted that such an ill wind might well precede armed conflict of epic proportion.

Years later, he wrote in his *War Memoirs,*

> When I was an adolescent, what happened to France interested
> me beyond anything else, whether it was a matter of history or
> the struggle of public life. I therefore watched the drama that
> was, without a pause, being acted in the forum, with pleasure but
> also with severity. All the more so since at the beginning of the
> century there appeared the premonitory symptoms of the war.
> I must admit that in my first youth I imagined this unknown
> adventure without horror and glorified it in advance. In short,
> I did not doubt that France would go through enormous trials,
> that the whole point of life consisted of one day rendering her
> some conspicuous service, and that I should have the opportunity
> of doing so.[6]

After two months of study in Belgium, he wrote to his father,

> I have had a great misfortune this week. In mathematics examina-
> tion we had on the twentieth, I was twelfth. Then, since luck is not
> with me this month I have just been marked second in physics and
> chemistry. I still read a great deal of history and natural history,
> and above all a great deal of German. They read us an account of
> the latest fighting on the Algerian frontier. Lieutenant de Saint-
> Hilaire of the Tirailleurs, who was killed in action, is the cousin of
> one of the boys here and it seems that he was an old boy of the rue
> des Postes.[7]

De Gaulle was struck by the death of a French officer defending
the reaches of the empire, the soldier not only related to a current
schoolmate but who had attended a school where Henri had taught.
Truly, de Gaulle had already come to the realization that the foundation of France, its seat of power, lay in the twin pillars of the Catholic
Church and the army. He had devoted his life to the military, and
from his earliest days the influence of the church was ever present
within him. Each of these was a stabilizing and lasting institution
within the country, and the church was the instrument of Almighty

God, who without doubt guided the destiny of France and his own as well.

By the time Charles had reached his teens, a sense of purpose had begun to solidify within him. His professors had seen glimpses of brilliance but warned that the young student might squander his gifts with the passage of time rather than seize the opportunity which lay before him. They need not have worried.

As other world leaders were to discover in the years to come, when Charles de Gaulle became fixed upon a course of action to achieve a desired outcome, he applied intellect and energy. The cost must be borne in the process. An innate belief in himself and a sense of destiny that later manifested as something altogether similar to the Divine Right of Kings laid bare an aloof and cold exterior, a dour countenance which neither suffered fools nor warmly hailed a close friend. Perhaps in solitude he found strength and cultivated the resolution to pursue his own ambitions and those of France without faltering.

He once wrote that his life had been consumed since adolescence with the realization that "the interest in life consisted in one day rendering France some signal service and that I would have occasion to do so."[8]

While he might well have followed his father and become a teacher, or even decided to follow his religious upbringing and enter the priesthood, neither seems to have rivaled the call of the military for Charles. A note of irony must be acknowledged in the young man's career decision. Despite the fact that a regimented life and the necessity of taking orders from others would seem the antithesis of his natural inclination, there was also a great appeal in the perceived order of things that the army could provide. There would no doubt be opportunity to command and to display personal bravery, while there could be no nobler undertaking than that of a defender of France. He was, after all, a leader.

Once he had decided to apply for admission to the prestigious military academy at St. Cyr, Charles threw himself into his studies with renewed vigor. Founded by Napoleon Bonaparte, St. Cyr had been a training ground for many French officers who had fought in the emperor's wars of conquest on the continent of Europe. Steeped in tradition, the academy was a bastion of the old school, whose primary doctrine of military conduct was to maintain the offensive at all costs.

Realizing that his prowess in French history and a keen knowledge of the military operations of the nation's great soldiers were not enough, de Gaulle pursued high marks in mathematics, science, and other disciplines that were prerequisites to success in the entrance examination. In the autumn of 1908, he entered the College Stanislas intent upon mastering mathematics and science in order to ensure his acceptance to St. Cyr.

Early in his first term, it appeared that Charles might once again prove only mediocre in his studies, finishing eighteenth in a class of 29 students. However, by the spring he steadily climbed to a rank of second.

In the late summer of 1909, Charles went to the seaside town of Wimereux to rest after two years of intense study. However, there was no rest to be had. The results of his entrance examination to St. Cyr would be available any day.

Finally, on September 30, the young man received word that he had been accepted. Of 800 hopefuls, 221 had been considered worthy for admission on the strength of the challenging test. De Gaulle stood 119th among them. While it may not have been an auspicious beginning, the die had been cast. Interestingly, a new regulation had recently been passed by the French military establishment. All officer candidates were required to spend a year in the rank and file of the army—in order to learn how to be led prior to leading soldiers themselves.

Near his hometown of Lille, the 33rd Infantry Regiment was headquartered at Arras. De Gaulle enlisted on October 10, 1909, was assigned to the 5th Company, and began a lifelong relationship of love and hate with the French military. Private de Gaulle towered above the other soldiers at six feet five inches. His large nose was his most prominent facial feature and often attracted as much attention as his great height. The new recruit was immediately an object of curiosity among his fellow soldiers. The combination of his physical countenance and his often obstinate personality did not seem to suit de Gaulle for the barracks life, nor for the archaic practices and seemingly pointless instruction of an army in the doldrums.

While de Gaulle understood the importance of discipline and drill in order for soldiers to act in coordination and follow necessary orders on the battlefield, the outmoded methods and dated doctrine wasted time and even seemed to dampen the enthusiasm of those who would be responsible for leading the army during the tumultuous years to come. As he labored to remain in step while marching, his thoughts were moving swiftly forward in an entirely different cadence.

Charles de Gaulle, born to lead, was without doubt challenged by the requirement to follow. He was continually at odds with his sergeant, who seemed to personify the ineffective, dull-witted automatons who populated the ranks and stifled the innovation and élan that made an army effective. The response to inept authority was a matter of course for de Gaulle, and he would follow his own sense of what was right throughout his life. From time to time, he was bound to pay a price, whether enduring the wrath of a noncommissioned officer or stubbornly maintaining the interests of his country among the heads of powerful nations, when he was virtually alone in doing so. De Gaulle's self-assurance and personal conviction were enough to convince him to stay the course.

Inspection time was often the source of comic relief for the other recruits who lined the barracks as the sergeant strode in. At the sound of his name, de Gaulle answered and the war of wits was on. Crumpled field packs, disheveled clothing, and various aspects of the living area far from being prepared to the expected standard would elicit a poke of the sergeant's walking stick. Items that were stored overhead would then cascade to the floor.

Despite his setbacks, he was promoted to the rank of corporal in the spring of 1910. His company commander, identified as Captain de Tugny, declined to elevate Charles above that grade, and when asked why de Gaulle had not been promoted during the year, the exasperated captain responded, "What use to make that young man a sergeant when the only military title that would interest him would be Grand Constable?"[9] Self-doubt was foreign to de Gaulle, and obedience to authority that was naturally flawed ran counter to his very being.

The reference was to what had for centuries been the highest rank in the French army. The assessment was reasonably accurate. For Charles de Gaulle, there was no position except that of command. The French army might be commanded by a cadre of misguided old men living in the past; however, in time the situation would change dramatically—or so de Gaulle intended.

Aside from those deficiencies that were readily apparent to the common French soldier, the army still bore the stigma of defeat in the Franco-Prussian War. The French military had been forced to back down from the brink of war in the face of superior British forces at Fashoda in 1898, as both nations sought to rapidly expand their colonial empires in East Africa.

In addition, the scandalous Dreyfus Affair hung like a pall over the organization, creating distrust and doubt within the officer corps, jeopardizing its credibility, and potentially undermining its ability to command. Alfred Dreyfus had been a lieutenant of artillery in the French army. In the autumn of 1894, largely on the basis of falsified documents and other trumped up evidence, he was tried and convicted on charges of spying for Germany. Subsequently, he was stripped of his rank and banished to the penal colony at Devil's Island in French Guiana. Because of his Jewish descent and his birth in the border province of Alsace, Dreyfus appeared a likely individual to perpetrate such a crime against the state. However, two years later it was discovered that another officer had actually committed the offense.

A major cover-up ensued, with the guilty party standing trial and being found innocent. Meanwhile, the highest echelons of the French army suppressed evidence and Dreyfus languished in prison. The Dreyfus Affair festered and then, with the publication of an article titled *J'accuse* by the author Émile Zola that appeared in the Paris newspaper *L'Aurore,* it became an open wound. Largely on the basis of Zola's writings, Dreyfus was brought back from Devil's Island to stand trial a second time. The public nature of the scandal divided not only the command structure of the French army but also the whole of French society. In the end, Dreyfus was exonerated. However, long after the affair had technically ended antagonism among those French officers who had supported Dreyfus and those who had wrongly accused him smoldered. Dreyfus, it turns out, had been the victim of both anti-Semitism and the criminal refusal of once trusted French officers to right an apparent wrong.

The specter of the Dreyfus Affair haunted the French army for decades and may well have influenced the conduct and preparedness of the military force during two world wars, one that bled France white and another which led to its brutal occupation by the Nazis. Distrust among the leadership of the army impeded the cohesive direction of the military for decades. Although de Gaulle rarely mentioned the Dreyfus Affair, he did write of its effect upon his psyche in later years, while also commenting on several other events of his youth.

"Nothing affected me more," he commented in his *War Memoirs,* "than the evidence of our national successes: Popular enthusiasm when the Czar of Russia passed through a review at Longchamp, the marvels of the Exhibition, the first flights of our aviators. Nothing saddened me more profoundly than our weaknesses and our mistakes, as revealed to my childhood gaze by the way people looked at the things they said: the surrender at Fashoda, the Dreyfus case, social conflicts, religious strife. As an adolescent, the fate of France, whether as a subject of history or the stake in public life, interested me above everything."[10]

De Gaulle was indeed profoundly affected by these events. Interestingly, a facet of French foreign policy was a by-product of the incident at Fashoda. Known as the Fashoda Syndrome, this political position asserts that France must always remain on guard against the influence of Great Britain.

Perhaps Charles de Gaulle's vision of the grandeur of France was somehow dependent upon vigilance against a preeminent Britain nearly to the extent that it was also concerned with defense against a militaristic Germany. Indeed, throughout his life de Gaulle may be seen as embracing the British as allies while also holding them at arm's length with mistrust.

Such was the state of the French army, bruised, somewhat vulnerable, and perhaps a microcosm of French society as a whole at the dawn of the twentieth century. Doubtless, as Charles de Gaulle stood poised to enter the military academy at St. Cyr, he was already feeling the perpetual pull of destiny, influenced by the patriotic pride and scholarly sway of his parents, the sweep of 30 years of recent history, and the certainty that he would one day become the guardian of France's national honor.

"All my life I have had a certain idea of France," he later wrote in his memoirs. "This is inspired by sentiment as much as by reason. The emotional side of me tends to imagine France, like the princess in the fairy stories or the Madonna in the frescoes, as dedicated to an exalted and exceptional destiny. Instinctively, I have the feeling that Providence has created her either for complete successes or for exemplary misfortunes. If, in spite of this, mediocrity shows in her acts and deeds, it strikes me as an absurd anomaly, to be imputed to the faults of Frenchmen, not to the genius of the land. But the positive side of my mind assures me that France is not really herself unless in the front rank; that only vast enterprises are capable of counterbalancing the ferments of dispersal which are inherent in her people; that our country, as it is, surrounded by the others, as they are, must aim high and hold itself straight, on pain of mortal danger. In short, to my mind, France cannot be France without greatness."[11]

Young Charles de Gaulle not only knew the greatness of France; he was also beginning to glimpse greatness within himself.

CHAPTER 2

Crucible of War

FOLLOWING THE OBLIGATORY YEAR IN THE RANKS, CHARLES DE GAULLE entered the hallowed halls of St. Cyr, on the outskirts of Paris near Versailles, during a heavy rain on October 14, 1910. As tradition demands, the newest of the military trainees received a somewhat trying welcome from upperclassmen.

In a brief letter to his father the day after his arrival, he wrote, "I had reckoned on being able to write you a letter after dinner, but the seniors who have been here these four days past spent this time in giving us lectures, and in persecuting us too, though not viciously."[1]

While his nickname of the Grand Constable seems to have followed him from his year with the 33rd Infantry Regiment, de Gaulle's imposing height quickly became the object of derision from his fellow students. He earned a variety of additional nicknames.

"The Big Asparagus" referred to his height, elongated forehead, and pronounced nose. "Mr. Two Yards" was roughly equivalent to the French reference to the high-jump event in track and field, and "Le Coq" may well have been a grudging tribute to his apparent lack of concern about the harassment. A traditional symbol of France, the fighting cock nickname may even have pleased him somewhat. It is also possible that by the time he neared his twentieth birthday he had already heard many similar taunts. In fact, he had turned them to his advantage, often reciting long comic passages from the popular play *Cyrano de Bergerac* by Edmond Rostand, in which the hero has a large nose.

Yet Charles de Gaulle seemed always to keep his distance from others and cultivated few lasting friendships during his days at St. Cyr. Although he became acquainted with a number of the future leaders of the French army, he preferred his own company, remaining aloof from classmates as he did from most others in his lifetime.

Once again, Charles's initial academic effort seems to have been somewhat less than remarkable. On one of his papers, an instructor noted, "Average in everything except height."[2]

While such a comment may have strictly related to classroom performance, it may also have been in reaction to the austere countenance that the young cadet displayed. Nevertheless, Charles did set out to excel, studying dutifully and improving his class standing to forty-fifth by the end of his first year. By far the outstanding member of the class was Alphonse Juin, who later became a Marshal of France. He was seriously wounded during World War I, served with distinction during World War II, and opposed independence for Algeria decades later, moving de Gaulle to press for Juin's retirement from the military.

By the time he reached graduation on October 1, 1912, de Gaulle ranked thirteenth in a class of 211. Throughout the years at St. Cyr, he maintained a keen awareness of the necessity of military training and discipline. However, he often questioned his instructors and expressed his opinions freely. Without question, such a willingness to disagree with authority would hinder his progress through the ranks of the French army's officer corps in the years to come. In contrast, it may have been the single most significant personality trait in his rise to power during the dark days of 1940.

In the St. Cyr magazine, a sketch of Charles in the classroom was accompanied by a caption that seemed almost prophetic in its description of the scene. "The St. Syrien de Gaulle undergoing an oral in history: the examiner is in a tight corner," it read.[3]

A review of his academic record reveals a strong performance overall. A captain's report noted, "Conduct Faultless; Manners Very Good; Intelligence Very lively and quick; Upbringing Carefully attended to; Character Upright; Attitude Very fine; Zeal Very sustained; Military spirit Highly developed; Physical appearance Agreeable; Power of marching Very good; Resistance to fatigue Great."

The report continued with the following narrative assessment:

> General estimate: A very highly gifted cadet. Conscientious and earnest worker. Excellent state of mind. Calm and energetic nature. Will make an excellent officer. Report of the major in command of infantry exercises: A thorough soldier, much attached to the service, very conscientious. Calm and forceful in command. Will make an excellent officer. General appreciation by the officer commanding the school: Has made continual progress since his joining the school, has a great deal in the way of abilities, energy, zeal, enthusiasm, and power of command and decision. Cannot fail to make an excellent officer.

His progress appears nothing short of remarkable. Yet it provides an insight into the character of de Gaulle that would serve to confound his fellow officers, political opponents, and even allies in the years to come. In the army, the young soldier was willing to accept a certain degree of regimentation as a means to an end—the opportunity to express his opinion. Whether that opinion ruffled feathers or crushed toes seemed to have mattered little. Truth, superior analytical thinking, and that overwhelming sense of destiny would vindicate conduct which tried the patience of others. Therefore, while obedience and discipline were required of other soldiers, de Gaulle believed it to be his duty to question authority, to assert his point of view, and to win the day through perseverance. Close relations with other individuals, and later other nations, were most often seen as a necessity to advance the agenda of de Gaulle, and therefore the agenda of France.

While the cavalry might well have been considered a more elite branch of the army, Charles chose to return to the infantry upon graduation. Interestingly, he further chose to return to Arras and his old outfit, the 33rd Infantry Regiment. He was familiar with the unit—although it had undoubtedly changed since his original departure—and there was the possibility that returning as an officer might engender a bit more respect than he had received while in the enlisted ranks. One other possibility for his choice of unit is plausible. He may have already heard of its current commander, Colonel Philippe Pétain, who had come to the regiment in the spring of 1911.[4]

Pétain, whose greatest and worst days were still ahead of him, had already gained quite a reputation as a military theorist and lecturer, and beyond that, as a tactician who was willing to challenge the prevailing sentiment that continuing attack was superior to the massing of firepower that could be concentrated and that would precede a rapid advance through a breach in the enemy lines. De Gaulle may well have been familiar with Pétain and was drawn to the military man with the makings of a first-rate mentor.

In the presence of officers who outranked him, young Second Lieutenant de Gaulle remained outspoken, ready to thrust and parry during discussions ranging from philosophy to battlefield tactics. Although Pétain took note of this upstart junior officer and watched his progress from the moment de Gaulle took command of his squad, one early encounter is emblematic of a mutually beneficial and eventually tragic, warm and then terribly cold, association that was to span more than three decades.

Once, as Colonel Pétain held court with a group of officers, lecturing on the Battle of Arras fought in 1654 by the armies of the Vicomte de Turenne and the Prince de Condé, Pétain was said to have asserted forcefully that de Condé, who eventually lost the battle, had actually proven superior to Turenne in his decision making in the heat of the fight. As most of the officers nodded in agreement, one of their number dared to speak up.

"But, Colonel, no!" blurted de Gaulle from across the crowded room. "Surely, colonel, the proof of the tactical skill is in the eventual result. You argue that Condé was right not to try to outflank Hocquincourt after capturing La Ferté. But the answer is that the firepower of Turenne was so great and so well handled that Condé was persuaded not to persist in the engagement, and thus Arras was saved."

Pétain was somewhat taken aback but probably not totally surprised by the outburst. "Stand up, Lieutenant de Gaulle," he said tersely. "Lieutenant, you have obviously studied your Siege of Arras very thoroughly. I applaud your diligence. We must talk over the lessons of this battle again some time."[5]

From that day on the colonel and the young lieutenant were often seen in each other's company, sometimes heavily engaged in conversation. The two agreed that the face of modern war was changing. Advances in technology might soon enough render time-honored tactics as a needless waste of fine infantry.

Although the two officers became close, de Gaulle maintained his obstinate perspective and his conviction of his own virtual infallibility. On Bastille Day in 1913, Pétain actually had de Gaulle arrested when troops supposedly under his command broke ranks during inspection, although de Gaulle believed it had been the mistake of another officer. It was customary for de Gaulle to visit Paris on Sundays; however, it appeared that confinement would prevent any travel plans for the week. Pétain must have reconsidered, however, since he eventually lifted all disciplinary actions.

De Gaulle ran to the nearby station and leaped aboard the train just as the wheels began to gather momentum. Coincidentally, he stepped into the same railway car that Pétain, dressed in civilian clothes, was occupying. The colonel commented, "So, young man, you almost missed the train?" To which de Gaulle responded, "Yes, colonel, but I was sure I would catch it." Pétain blurted, "But you were under arrest." Then de Gaulle concluded, "That is true, but since the penalty was unjust, I was sure you would lift it."[6]

Both Pétain and de Gaulle believed that France was ill prepared to fight another war with Germany or to protect her vital interests around the globe, particularly in North Africa. Just as the rifle had rendered the musket obsolete in the nineteenth century, the recent invention of the machine gun and the increasing caliber of heavy artillery would prove devastating during the wars of the future. Further, there were ominous signs that another war, on an unprecedented scale, might well be initiated within a few years. For what it was worth, most of the officers in the French army may have indeed agreed that war would come, and soon. However, paths diverged when theoretical discussion turned to the prospective conduct of that war, particularly in the deployment of tanks, artillery, and infantry on the battlefield.

In an address to the Army General Staff at the École Supériere de Guerre prior to the summer of 1914, when Europe was plunged into the horror of World War I, Pétain dared to assail the dominant school of thought, which favored the construction of strong fortifications for the prosecution of a decidedly defensive war. "Let us first crush the enemy by artillery fire," he advocated, "and afterward we shall win our victory. An offensive is gunfire leading an advance. A defensive is gunfire stopping an advance. The gun wins ground. The infantry occupies it."[7]

As the protégé of Pétain, an officer who maintained the respect of those who opposed him, de Gaulle would benefit greatly from the association. His patron did, in fact, save the young officer's military career on more than one occasion. To some, Pétain was preaching heresy and helping to slowly erode the esprit de corps that underpinned the rank and file of the French army. He did, however, cultivate his devotees, and de Gaulle was one of them to a great extent, adhering to Pétain's philosophy but urgently insisting (to a greater degree than his mentor) that rapid movement was as critical to victory on the battlefield as firepower.

"One must have the offensive spirit," de Gaulle warned an audience of soldiers. "This means that one must in all places and at all times have one single idea, that of advancing. As soon as the fighting begins everybody in the French army, the commanding general, the chiefs and the soldiers have only one idea left—advancing, advancing to the attack, reaching the Germans so as to split them or make them run away."[8]

Given the general attitude of the French army, that one day another war with Germany would redress the losses sustained in the Franco-Prussian War, de Gaulle seems to have had no difficulty recognizing the growing tension between the two countries. At the time this discourse was delivered, World War I was less than a year away. The army would become the instrument of the restoration of French honor, and de Gaulle was convinced that he would make a significant contribution to the endeavor. Four months before the outbreak of hostilities, he told the assembled officers of the 3rd Battalion, 33rd Infantry Regiment that the Germans outnumbered the defenders along the French frontier. He praised the equipment and training of the Germans but also asserted that French artillery was of superior quality and ended his presentation with a confident statement that the French army would ultimately be victorious.

Nearly a half century later, de Gaulle wrote in his memoirs of the lasting impression that Pétain had made. "My first colonel showed me the meaning of the gift and art of command."[9] The regimental commander was detached, not given to shows of emotion, and rarely spoke at length. He was distant from those under his command yet incredibly aware of issues, concerns, and morale. As de Gaulle developed, he took this command presence to heart and sought to emulate it. By 1914, Pétain was already in his late fifties. Contemporaries had long passed him by in rank and perceived importance. Controversial views had cost him regular promotions, and now he was nearing the age of retirement. However, to de Gaulle he seemed to hold something of a moral authority, a higher ground that would be proven correct in time.

As a junior officer, de Gaulle was exceptional in wearing the mantle of command. He was always impeccably dressed in a spotless uniform. He expected subordinates to show proper military etiquette, once reprimanding a soldier for not rendering the proper salute and informing the soldier's commanding officer that such a lack of courtesy should be addressed more fully with his charges. He made it his business to know the soldiers he led, their backgrounds, strengths and weaknesses, and he was reported to have committed their service records to memory.

De Gaulle regularly addressed his men with lengthy discourses on the meaning of duty and honor, the proud traditions of the French army and of the nation. "You are now no longer ordinary men: you have become soldiers," he once told them.

Have you already wondered why? France is a nation. But is she the only nation in the world? No! There are other nations that ask nothing better than to conquer us, to stop us speaking French and to take away our freedom. So France has provided herself with an army; she has decided that each of her sons should come and serve her in his turn, and here you are! It is 42 years now that France has been at peace and if foreigners choose to declare war on her, they will find someone to answer them, I can tell you. From now on our land, our houses, and our children shall remain ours. And then France has not only enemies abroad to fear. At home there are often people who look for an opportunity to foster trouble and prevent good citizens from living in peace.

And who can tell whether this very year may not be decisive for the country's future? I do not have to tell you that the situation abroad looks more threatening than ever. Let us reflect that tomorrow's victory may depend on each one of us.[10]

When de Gaulle's first year in the regiment was over, Pétain enthusiastically recommended his promotion to first lieutenant, writing, "Very intelligent, passionately devoted to his profession. Handled his section perfectly on maneuvers. Worthy of all praise."[11]

When Pétain penned an assessment of the lieutenant's performance, it was, perhaps, the closest the old colonel had ever come to gushing over a subordinate. He wrote for de Gaulle's file, "Has proved from the beginning to be an officer of real worth who raises high hopes for the future. Throws his whole heart into his job as an instructor. Gave a brilliant lecture on the causes of the conflict in the Balkan Peninsula."[12]

At long last, in the summer of 1914, the assassination of Archduke Franz Ferdinand and Austria-Hungary's subsequent declaration of war on Serbia ignited world war as tangled alliances compelled the great powers of Europe to mobilize. When Germany declared war on France on August 3, the 33rd Infantry Regiment, with de Gaulle commanding the 11th Company, had already been preparing for some time. By now Pétain had been elevated to higher command and left the regiment. De Gaulle found time to assess the state of affairs on the eve of battle, writing, "Absolute calm on the part of the troops and the population. But uneasiness on many faces. What important men the officers are now."[13]

In his 1938 book *La France et Son Armée,* or *France and Its Army,* published a full 20 years after World War I had ended, de Gaulle remembered that the opening of hostilities had been greeted with euphoria. "Not a single group to protest against the mobilization. Not a single strike to interfere with it. Not a single vote in parliament to refuse the war credits."[14]

This was tempered with the acknowledgment that "Tactically, the realization of German firepower made nonsense of the current military doctrines. Morally, all the people's illusions, with which they had steeled themselves, went up in smoke.... Between 20 and 23 August a perfect sense of security was turned into a frantic sense of danger."[15]

Reservists were incorporated into the ranks, letters were written home, and the soldiers packed up and prepared to advance toward an uncertain future. De Gaulle seemed to grasp the reality of the trial that was to come, at least momentarily putting aside the romance, honor, and glory of war upon which his efforts had been fixed for several years. He wrote, "Goodbye, my rooms, my books, my familiar objects. How much more intense life does seem, and how the smallest trifles stand out in relief when perhaps everything may be coming to an end."[16]

The 33rd Infantry Regiment was considered one of the best in the army, and its initial assignment was to move from Arras northward to defend against a great German offensive intended to sweep through neutral Belgium, pivot to the south, and drive deep into the heart of France. In less than two weeks, the regiment had entered the Ardennes Forest, crossed into Belgium, and advanced to the town of Dinant. The Germans were moving through Belgium as well, and their aircraft kept watch on the dispositions of the French troops below.

Two weeks after his baptism of fire, Charles wrote of the hours preceding the intense fight for control of a key bridge across the river Meuse at Dinant.

Night march. Everyone feels we are going into battle, but everyone is determined and in high spirits. The enemy no longer occupies Dinant. We therefore enter the town. The men, all in, sleep lying in the street. Captain Bosquet and I sitting on chairs. At six in the morning, boom! boom! the music begins. The enemy shells Dinant furiously. These are the first shots of the campaign we have received. What was my impression? Why not say? Two seconds of physical emotion, a tightening of my throat. Then that was all. The men began looking serious, then banter came to the top again.[17]

Nothing validates the authority of a military officer more surely than courage under fire, and Lieutenant Charles de Gaulle set about making the most of his initial opportunity. It came on August 15, 1914. While the men of his 11th Company sought shelter from the German artillery fire in a nearby railroad cut adjacent to where the track bisected a roadway, their commander remained calm. He later commented, "I sat on a bench in the street and stayed there out of bravado. There was in fact no merit about it since I was not in any way alarmed."[18]

The German fire grew in intensity, and soon the order was received. The 11th Company was to fix bayonets, outpace the enemy, and hold the bridge.

"To reach my platoon I had to go over the level crossing," he remembered.

> I decided to cross at a walk. Lord, what a tingling in my legs! I shouted, 'First platoon, advance with me!' and I raced forward, knowing that our only chance of success was acting very fast. I had the feeling that at that moment my self split in two, the one running like an automaton and the other anxiously watching him. I had scarcely crossed the 20 yards that separated us from the beginning of the bridge when something struck my knee like a whiplash, making me trip. I fell, and Sergeant Debout fell on top of me, killed outright. Then there was an appalling hail of bullets all around me. I could hear the muffled sound of them hitting the dead and wounded scattered over the ground. I extricated myself from my neighbors, corpses or little better, and there I was crawling along the street under the same hail of bullets. How it came about that I was not riddled like a sieve during the passage will always be one of the great problems of my life.

> Limping and in a bad way, I dragged myself to the Meuse bridge. Our artillery was firing at a tremendous rate. It was high time! I

busied myself by gathering together what was left of the regiment at Dinant. Night fell; my task was over. The peasants organized the transport of the wounded in carts. I got into one of them.[19]

De Gaulle's platoon had attacked bravely but taken severe casualties during the event. Forced to take shelter in the houses of the village, those who survived the initial assault were withdrawn a short time later, their valiant charge leaving the company decimated. A harbinger of the modern warfare that was to come, the toll in French soldiers had doubtlessly been increased due to the orders of senior commanders who had yet to comprehend the logical fate which awaited infantrymen advancing in the open while under machine gun fire and without the preparation of an artillery bombardment.

The young lieutenant had suffered a bullet wound to the right fibula, the small bone in the lower leg, along with some nerve damage. He was first evacuated to the town of Charleroi, coincidentally where his sister Marie-Agnes happened to be living. He was then transported to Arras, and later to St. Joseph Hospital in Paris, where he underwent surgery, and finally he was to recover at Lyons. The convalescence was to require an agonizing seven months, during which Charles ruminated on his time in combat.

When he had recovered sufficiently to write, he observed thoughtfully, "The first clash is an immense surprise. In a moment it is clear that all the courage and valor in the world cannot prevail against gunfire." He later reflected, "I admit that in my first youth I pictured this unknown adventure with no horror and magnified it in anticipation."[20]

Exhibiting the ability to reach logical conclusions based on an intuitive understanding of relations between nations, a quality rarely seen in junior officers, Charles pondered the unfolding events on a grand scale. He asserted, "The British government bears a heavy responsibility for not making up their minds to go to war until the last minute and having their army very ill prepared," which was shortly followed by, "...our best interests require us not to lay down our arms until we have linked up with the Russians across Germany—otherwise we will have to start again in 10 years' time."[21]

The opening weeks of the war had gone decidedly against the French and the newly arrived British Expeditionary Force, the Germans continuing their offensive that had opened the war in the West and eventually reaching the outskirts of Paris. As he recovered, Charles followed the progress of the First Battle of the Marne and wrote to both his parents that the victory was bound to turn the tide of the war. The battle actually resulted in a stabilized front, and it contributed directly to the horror of trench warfare, which plagued both sides until the end of the war in 1918.

"Our dead must have quivered in their graves when they heard the victorious steps of our soldiers and the terrible rumbling of our guns," he told his father.

> France is coming to herself again. The generalissimo has at once cut the losses by not persisting in the decisive battle on the Meuse. He has chosen new terrain, escaping from the enemy's grip without a check and completely modifying the faulty disposition of his forces. On the Marne the fighting was much better coordinated. The enemy will not be able to halt our pursuit before the Meuse and Luxembourg, and we shall have all the glory of having beaten the army that thought itself the finest in the world in a great and decisive battle—and that without the Russians having been absolutely necessary to us.[22]

Typically, a request to return to one's former unit would have been denied. However, these were extraordinary times and the 33rd Infantry Regiment needed junior officers, its ranks depleted by combat. By the middle of October, de Gaulle had rejoined the 33rd. Since he had not fully recovered when he returned, the young officer was given a staff position. De Gaulle fumed at the idea of doing the paperwork of a regimental adjutant rather than leading troops in the field. He nagged and persisted in an effort to be allowed to lead reconnaissance patrols, and finally permission was granted.

De Gaulle led numerous patrols into the German lines, sometimes even eavesdropping on the enemy soldiers' conversations and bringing back prisoners for interrogation. Before long, he was mentioned in glowing terms in an order of the day issued by the 2nd Division. "Lieutenant Charles de Gaulle has carried out a series of reconnaissance missions of the enemy positions and has brought back with him information of the greatest value," it read.[23]

De Gaulle took time to note that the French government had not yet returned to Paris from Bordeaux, where it had fled when threatened by the German advance on the Marne during the autumn of 1914. He complained again that British reinforcements had reached the front too late, and was taken aback by what he considered to be a lack of fighting spirit among the French officer corps.

In November 1914, when German troops extended their trench line very near French positions, de Gaulle leaped at the opportunity to organize a patrol that would root them out of their forward post. This idea was quashed by senior officers who explained that such a provocation would undoubtedly result in retribution against their own soldiers. Therefore, such an offensive effort would be counterproductive. On another occasion, his platoon received a pair of new mortars, which de Gaulle dutifully prepared to fire against the Germans a few hundred yards away. Again, he was told to refrain from offensive action, since German artillery would no doubt reply and create casualties and general discomfort among the French troops. When Lieutenant de Gaulle fired the weapons anyway, his company was replaced in the line the following day.

Headstrong and resolute in the face of the enemy, Charles de Gaulle was not about to sit idly by while the enemy was close at hand and the opportunity to strike a blow was at his disposal. His disobedience in the field was characteristic of an unwavering sense of duty and foreshadowed his future conduct in both military and civilian affairs.

In January 1915, Charles was recognized for his bravery with the award of the Croix de Guerre, and early in February he was promoted to the temporary rank of captain. This rank was made permanent the following September. Meanwhile, casualties had begun to mount during the attrition of trench warfare. Although the exact date and nature of the event is somewhat obscure, it is known that de Gaulle sustained a second wound in combat, probably on March 15, 1915, at Mesnil-les-Hurlus. An apparent shrapnel wound in the left hand appeared to be minor at first. However, it became infected, and de Gaulle required hospitalization again to treat a grotesquely swollen forearm and a high fever. The wound nagged him for the rest of his life, later requiring him to wear his wedding ring on his right hand.

In October, de Gaulle was given command of the 10th Company of the 33rd Regiment. By the end of the year he had requested a transfer to the Verdun area, where the Germans were mounting a huge offensive and his mentor, now General Pétain, was in command. Colonel Emile Boudhors, commander of the 33rd Regiment, agreed somewhat reluctantly, noting, "In view of the gravity of the situation, and of the importance I attach to this mission, I believe that Captain de Gaulle alone is capable of accomplishing it."[24]

In fact, the entire 33rd Regiment was eventually ordered to Verdun. On February 25, 1916, the troops had arrived in the combat area after a weeklong transfer from the town of Nanteuil-la-Fosse. German progress threatened a breakthrough of the fortified lines at Verdun, and the 33rd was positioned in a highly active sector between the town of le Calvaire and Douaumont, where one of the largest fortifications in the French line, which many had believed impregnable, had only recently fallen into German hands.

On March 1, de Gaulle was ordered to lead a reconnaissance in force to determine the strength of German troops near the French lines and to ascertain the dispositions of supporting units on the left and right flanks of the 33rd Regiment. This was dangerous business, and de Gaulle was misinformed by an officer of the 110th Regiment, which the 33rd had been ordered to relieve, that the Germans had at least temporarily ceased offensive operations.

As he moved forward, de Gaulle observed the devastation caused by several days of concentrated artillery fire. Communications trenches had been obliterated, infrastructure had been destroyed, and even more alarming, it was clear that the Germans had been preparing to renew their attack. They were quickly occupying the fortress of Douaumont and positioning artillery and machine guns to sweep the French lines. Although he reported the situation to the commander of the 110th Regiment, his concerns were discounted.

Colonel Boudhors requested artillery support and prepared to defend the line, which he knew would surely receive a hammer blow from the attacking Germans. The 10th company of the 3rd Battalion, to which de Gaulle's command belonged, had been assigned to a sector near a church about half a mile from the German-occupied fortress. At 6:30 a.m. on March 2, the enemy guns began to thunder, hurling shells of various caliber and as large as 380mm.

The war history of the 33rd Regiment described the ensuing combat as the soldiers endured

terrible shelling by heavy artillery over the whole breadth of the sector and to a depth of three kilometers. The earth trembled without a pause; the noise was unbelievable. No liaison, either forward or to the rear, was possible; all telephone wires had been cut and any messenger sent out was a dead man. The last came back...wounded and said, "The Germans are 20 yards away," on the road from Douauamont to Fleury. Guns at the ready, we prepared to defend this approach road whatever the cost.

At about 1:15 in the afternoon, after a bombardment that had already cut the lines to pieces, the Germans launched their advance to encircle the 3rd Battalion. It was the 12th Company, on the left of the 10th, that bore the brunt of their attack. The first who were seen were Germans rushing down from the fort wearing French helmets. Major Cordonnier, who was behind the center of the 11th Company, cried "Do not fire: they are French!" and almost at once he fell wounded or killed by a bullet in the throat, while Sergeant Major Bacro shouted, "Fire away; they are Germans," himself shooting furiously. Soon the Germans were in the rear of the 10th Company.

It was then that this magnificent feat was performed. The 10th Company was seen to charge straight forward at the massed enemy reaching the village, engaging them in a terrible hand-to-hand struggle in which these brave men received blows from rifle butts and bayonets from every side until they were overpowered. Seeing itself completely surrounded, the 10th Company launched itself in a furious attack led by its commanding officer, Captain de Gaulle, charging close packed bodies of men, selling its life dearly and falling gloriously.[25]

The French line was breached near de Gaulle's position, leaving two pockets of resistance unable to support one another. Ordering the few soldiers around him to fix bayonets, the captain led these men through a communications trench in an attempt to rejoin the remnants of his unit. German soldiers were encountered almost immediately.

Sometime later, while a prisoner of the Germans, he wrote of the ordeal. "I had hardly gone 10 meters when I came on a group of Boches crouching in a shellhole," he remembered. "They saw me at the same moment, and one of them ran his bayonet into me. The thrust went through my map case and wounded me in the thigh. Another Boche shot my orderly dead. Seconds later a grenade exploded in front of my face, and I lost consciousness."[26]

Colonel Boudhors, who may actually have seen de Gaulle fall, wrote to the young officer's parents that Charles was presumed dead. The colonel also recommended de Gaulle for a posthumous award of the Legion of Honor and mentioned him in dispatches related to the day's action. "Although he (de Gaulle) had been badly wounded by a bayonet thrust after a furious hand-to-hand engagement, [he] organized a knot of resistance in which his men fought until all the ammunition was gone, the rifles were shattered and the unarmed defenders had fallen," wrote Boudhors.[27]

Just how close Boudhors was to the fighting is debatable, since he went on to assert that de Gaulle had been further incapacitated by the effects of poison gas. Later in life, the former commander of the 33rd Infantry Regiment became a staunch supporter of de Gaulle, perpetuating his story of that day in the trenches.

Pétain received the news of de Gaulle's likely death and embellished the circumstances further in his own official dispatches. The commanding officer's account reads, "When his battalion, having undergone extremely heavy shelling, was decimated and when the Germans were reaching his company on all sides, Captain de Gaulle, a company commander well known for his great intellectual and moral value, led his men in a furious charge and a fierce hand-to-hand engagement, the only solution he considered compatible with military honor. Fell in the fighting. An incomparable officer in all respects."[28]

While neither story may have been entirely correct, one conclusion is indisputable. Captain Charles de Gaulle had exhibited extraordinary personal courage during the fighting at Douaumont and sustained his third combat wound in less than two years of service. In three days of intense combat, nearly two-thirds of the soldiers of the 33rd Infantry Regiment had been killed or wounded. Such horrific casualties, however, were typical on both sides, and combined casualties suffered during the ten-month ordeal at Verdun were in excess of a million men.

Despite his injury, de Gaulle did survive the battle of March 2, 1916, evacuated from the area by German soldiers, one of whom he was reported to have been fighting hand to hand when he suffered the bayonet wound. He regained consciousness while lying among the bodies of the dead in a small cart. Initially taken to Pierrepont, he received medical care at a German hospital in Mainz, and within two weeks he was well enough to travel with a bandaged left hip to another camp at Neisse.

Six weeks after he was wounded, he was able to write to his sister and inform her that he was indeed alive. This was followed by a letter to his father in July 1916, bemoaning his condition. "For a French officer, the state of being a prisoner is the worst of all," he wrote.

By the time this letter was written, the first of de Gaulle's five escape attempts had already been discovered and thwarted, resulting in a transfer to the penal camp at Szczucin, Lithuania, far from the Western Front. The conditions at Szczucin were abhorrent, and the prisoners were sheltered in a dismal old sawmill. Before his transfer, de Gaulle had devised an implausible plan to slip away and sail a small boat down the Danube River and into the Black Sea.

Frustrated but undaunted, he was determined to escape and joined with a lieutenant colonel named Tardiu and another officer, Lieutenant Roederer, to dig a tunnel. When the entrance was discovered, the punishment was transfer to a maximum security prison, Fort IX at Ingolstadt on the banks of the Danube in Bavaria. De Gaulle spent 120 days in solitary confinement. The prison itself was imposing, appearing to be built right into the side of a hill. A heavy iron door barred the exit from the main building, and beyond was a moat 15 yards wide and up to 6 feet deep. High walls enclosed the grounds, which were situated on something of an earthen mound up to 60 feet high.

Among de Gaulle's fellow prisoners at Ingolstadt were Colonel Georges Catroux, who would rise to the rank of general and become a stalwart of the Free French movement in 1940; Roland Garros, the aviation pioneer who developed a mechanism for forward firing machine guns mounted on the engine cowling of an aircraft and revolutionized aerial warfare; and Russian officer Mikhail Tukhachevsky, who would later achieve the rank of marshal and be executed during Josef Stalin's bloody purges of the Red Army officer corps during the 1930s.

Although most of the 150 prisoners held at Ingolstadt were pre-occupied with escape, de Gaulle pursued the activity with exceptional energy. He surveyed the security of the prison and was dismayed to see that a direct escape attempt was virtually impossible. One opportunity, however, did present itself. Outside the prison was a small hospital that served the German soldiers posted in the area along with some prisoners who had been wounded in battle. Charles decided that admission to the hospital for treatment would facilitate his escape.

Worried for her son, Madame de Gaulle had sent picric acid for Charles to use on areas of his body that had been irritated and swollen from exposure to the moist cold at the prison. He swallowed the skin preparation and the following day presented himself to the prison medical officer with what appeared to be a severe case of jaundice, including yellow eyes and cloudy urine. Once in the hospital, he met Captain Ducret, another prisoner intent on escaping.

The two took advantage of a local Frenchman who had apparently been impressed by the Germans to work as an electrician. This man supplied them with ample food, while the two prisoners bribed the German whose responsibility it was to transfer patients from an annex where they slept to the main hospital building. The German provided them with a map of the surrounding area, and once they had the map de Gaulle and Ducret coerced him into further cooperation, threatening to turn him over to the authorities for court martial if he did not provide them with German military caps and eventually his own uniform trousers.

On October 29, 1916, Ducret dressed as a male nurse and assisted the disguised de Gaulle out of the hospital and to freedom. Eluding the authorities for eight days, the pair made for the Swiss frontier and the town of Schaffhausen, nearly 200 miles away. However, heavy rainfall and the difficulties inherent with living on the run began to take their toll.

"On Sunday 5 November, the eighth day of our escape," remembered Charles, we reached Pfaffenhoffen, a small town 30 kilometers southwest of Ulm, having traveled two-thirds of our journey. We thought we should pass through without trouble. But it was Sunday. When we reached the central square, which was very well lit, we suddenly found ourselves in a crowd of young people of the town, who were fooling about in the streets. A week of living rough had given us the look of gallows birds, and we were noticed at once. We were arrested and taken to the town lockup.[29]

During the following eight months, Charles decided to postpone further escape attempts. He would allow the closer scrutiny he had been receiving from the prison guards to die down. He worked to improve his command of the German language, read books from the library, kept up with the progress of the war through newspapers that were provided to the prisoners, taught French to his friend Tukhachevsky, and began to openly discuss the conduct of military operations with his fellow prisoners, many of whom were officers who outranked the confident captain.

De Gaulle developed a series of lectures that became the basis for his short book *La Discorde chez l'Ennemi,* or *Discord among the Enemy,* a discussion of the German civilian government, its interaction with the nation's military establishment, and its influence on the conduct of the Great War, while also criticizing the strategic decisions made by some high-ranking German officers. The book was published in 1924 and proved an insightful appraisal of the German defeat, revealing de Gaulle's uncanny talent in assessing the strengths and weaknesses of both individuals and nations.

Further, the young officer pondered the meaning of character and deportment while in prison. Among notes written during this time was the following:

One must be a man of character. The way to succeed in action is to be capable of self mastery at all times. To be more precise, it is an indispensable condition of success. Self mastery should become a kind of habit, a reflex created by constant exercise of the will, in small matters as well: dress, conversation, direction of thought, a methodical carefully worked out approach in everything, particularly in one's work. To talk little is an absolute necessity.... And in action one must say nothing. The leader is the man who does not talk.[30]

De Gaulle held true to his own advice. Years later, foreign diplomats were often dumbfounded by his lack of verbal communication, and his subordinates remembered him as a man of few words.

After several months of good behavior, de Gaulle and a few other habitual offenders were transferred to a more picturesque facility at Rosenberg, in Franconia. In the autumn of 1917, four of them had once again conspired and executed an escape, along with a fifth officer who had arrived at the prison on the very day of the attempt and asked to go along.

The primary challenge this time was in negotiating the sheer rock wall on which the prison itself, a building dating to the sixteenth century, had been constructed. However, in a short time, the escaped prisoners were again on their way in the direction of Schaffhausen, this time half again as far as it had been from Ingolstadt, a distance of roughly 300 miles.

De Gaulle wrote, "After 10 days march in the direction of Schaffhausen we were worn out with cold and fatigue, and we had the unfortunate idea of sheltering for the day in a dovecote that stood by itself in the middle of the fields. Peasants working nearby heard us and alerted a soldier who was guarding the Russian prisoners working at a neighboring farm. When night fell, the soldier and some civilians surrounded the dovecote and called us to come down. We were obliged to obey."[31]

Less than a week after their recapture, de Gaulle and a companion decided on another escape attempt, this time sawing through a steel bar that covered the small window in their cell. They disguised themselves with civilian clothes and fake moustaches, managed to elude the guards, slipped down the cliffside once again, and reached the railroad station at Lichtenfels. As they attempted to board a train for Aachen, near the border with the Netherlands, they were once again apprehended.

This time, the punishment for repeated escape attempts was a return to Ingolstadt, where Charles spent the last two months of 1917 in solitary confinement, a dark cell with no reading material and no other diversions except a half hour of exercise per day. As the war progressed, prison life at Ingolstadt had become even harsher than before. A French officer was shot while trying to escape, and tensions ran high between the prisoners and their guards. A grievance was filed, and to defuse the situation the notorious prison was closed. De Gaulle was transferred through a fortress at Prinz Karl to the prison at Wülzburg, where he characteristically attempted another escape. After donning a stolen German uniform and being escorted out of the prison by the facility's French chaplain, he was recaptured a day later.

His final attempt to escape came only weeks before the signing of the armistice of November 11, 1918. De Gaulle concealed himself in a laundry basket. Once outside the compound, he made his way to Nuremberg, purchased a train ticket to Frankfurt, and took his seat. Shortly thereafter, he was stricken by a stomach virus and unable to continue the journey. He was returned to Wülzburg and waited out the remainder of the war.

When peace finally came, de Gaulle and many other prisoners were transferred to Passau, then Magdeburg, and finally Ludwigshafen. By mid-December he had reach Geneva, Switzerland, and subsequently Lyons, Paris, and his country homestead at La Ligerie, where the anxious family assembled to greet the war hero upon his return. His brothers, too, had survived the war. Perhaps this, in itself, was a miracle.

While still a prisoner in the spring of 1918, de Gaulle had become aware of the Michael Offensive, a massive German stroke that had been designed as a necessary, if not desperate, gamble to win the war. If successful, Germany might prevail before the full weight of the military and industrial power of the United States, which had entered the war in April 1917, could be brought to bear against it. General Erich Ludendorff, senior German commander in the West along with General Paul von Hindenburg, had sought a break in the Allied lines and a victorious march on Paris. However, the offensive was snuffed out at the Second Battle of the Marne, effectively ending the German effort.

When the Allies had experienced their initial setbacks during the Michael Offensive, de Gaulle had firmly believed in their resilience, although he also concluded that the war would drag on for some time to come. By the late summer, when victory seemed imminent against the despicable foe, de Gaulle found himself contemplating his own future. A state of near depression ensued.

He wrote to his mother from prison on September 1, 1918, and his somber tone would at first appear out of place. However, from the perspective of Charles de Gaulle his wartime experience had been a failure. The letter rings with lost opportunity.

"I am buried alive," he wrote.

> The other day I read in some paper that prisoners returning to France were called "ghosts." What aim can I have? My career, you say? But if I cannot get into the fighting again between now and the end of the war, shall I stay in the army? And what common-place kind of a future would I have there? Three years, four years of war in which I have not taken part: possibly more? The first, the essential condition for a future in the army, as far as officers of my age with some degree of ambition are concerned, will be to have gone through a campaign, to have learned how to judge it, to have molded one's reasoning, and to have tempered one's character and one's authority. From the military point of view I have no illusions. I, too, shall be no more than a "ghost."[32]

Characteristically, Charles de Gaulle had considered his 32 months of imprisonment a terrible misfortune, hardly befitting a man of destiny, one who would render great and memorable service to France. Three combat wounds, bravery under fire resulting in the award of several decorations, and multiple escape attempts that obliged the Germans to tie down men and other resources to keep him under control had counted for little. By the time he was 28 years old, Charles brooded about an uncertain future. If his own horizon was shrouded in doubt, then that of his beloved France might be as well.

On more than one occasion, de Gaulle exhibited bravery under fire, possibly driven by his desire to prove himself courageous or with that sense of destiny reassuring him that his time would not come before the completion of his personal mission to contribute to the glory of France. Once in 1915, while inspecting his company's positions in the trenches, de Gaulle and two lieutenants had come under German artillery fire. A mortar shell was seen headed directly for the three officers. De Gaulle stood erect, while the two lieutenants hugged the ground. When the shell passed overhead and crashed some distance to the rear, the two officers got back on their feet. "Gentlemen, were you afraid?" their captain wryly remarked.[33]

Regardless of his motivation, it is ironic that such an individual, fearless under fire, seemed despondent over the somewhat dismal prospects for future greatness. The absence of war was, somehow, working against him. Perhaps he remembered a conversation with Tukhachevsky while the two were prisoners.

The Russian had approached him at a time when de Gaulle seemed downcast. "Are you sad because the war is lost?" he asked the Frenchman. De Gaulle bellowed in reply, "The war is not lost! We have very nearly won it by now!" The Russian answered, "No, no! I meant are you sad because you are out of the war, because it is lost to you." Tukhachevsky then reasoned, "What good is it to be sad? The present may not be ours, but possibly the future will be."[34]

True enough, France emerged from World War I depleted of resources and with the brightest of a generation sacrificed in the horror of the trenches. Nevertheless, she and her allies had been victorious. France had her great heroes, but Charles de Gaulle was not among them. The fact that he had survived was apparently of little value in balancing his professional ledger. He had missed most of the greatest armed conflict the world had ever known. The opportunity to command troops and distinguish oneself through the exercise of military authority and acumen had evaporated.

De Gaulle, the professional soldier, was compelled to imagine a peacetime army, a nation tremendously fatigued by four years of war, and an unfulfilled future of mediocrity. How could such a gross miscarriage of justice be corrected? De Gaulle would be required to figure that out for himself.

CHAPTER 3

The Young Lion

In the wake of the First World War, Charles de Gaulle sought redemption. The despair evoked by his unrealized potential preyed upon his psyche; however, his resolution, fortitude, and personal will could not be extinguished. Aware of tactical military theory, advances in arms and equipment, and lessons learned in wartime he had missed while he was a prisoner of war, he set about making up for lost time.

Within days of his reunion with family at the country home in La Ligerie, de Gaulle learned that the French army had prepared a brief course of study at Saint-Maixent for officers who had been prisoners during the war. Its purpose was to familiarize them with all that had transpired, educating them with the latest information on modern warfare. After a few weeks with family, Charles eagerly packed off for school, absorbed the teaching and lectures, and filled in many of the gaps created by a near three-year absence, while regaining some measure of confidence in his future in the military.

De Gaulle saw the Allied victory in the recent war as principally a French victory. He hoped to see the leaders of his country, particularly Prime Minister Georges Clemenceau and Marshal Ferdinand Foch, previously the supreme commander of Allied forces on the Western Front, advocate harsh punishment for Germany and assert the primacy of France on the European continent.

"Like most of my countrymen," he wrote confidently to his father, "I finish the war brimming over with sentiments of generalized xenophobia and convinced that, in order to make ourselves respected, we must make a rational use of our military power, which is today the first in the world."[1]

Meanwhile, events in the East were unfolding to his advantage. With the defeat of Germany and Austria-Hungary, the map of Europe was once again being redrawn. In the process, some politicians and diplomats had advocated the reconstitution of an independent Poland, if for no other reason than to serve the West as a buffer against what they perceived as a dark and treacherous entity— Bolshevik Russia. The resurrected Poland, situated geographically between its traditional enemies of Russia and Germany (although the latter had been substantially weakened by military defeat), would need a standing army for defensive purposes.

Even as the guns of World War I fell silent, a Polish army of six divisions, consisting of expatriates, émigrés, and others rallying to the standard of the country, had been formed with the premise of moving from the West to Poland. Commanded by General Józef Haller, this army would be augmented by other troops from far and wide. Some of these Polish soldiers had fought for the Germans during World War I and had no misgivings about continuing to fight the Russians. Others had fought for the Russians and were no less conversely disposed. The United States and several nations of Western Europe supported the rise of a new Poland and the stability it might afford the fractured political and territorial landscape of the European continent.

France was becoming deeply involved in the situation, and even before he departed for Saint-Maixent, Charles had requested a posting to a cadre of French officers who would assist in molding the conglomeration of Polish soldiers into an army capable of defending the fledgling country. He saw an opportunity to distinguish himself once again as a leader of men, to demonstrate his abilities to inspire, to organize, and to command, and perhaps even to lead troops in battle. Though they might be Polish rather than French troops, the situation could still serve de Gaulle's postwar purpose.

The French and Polish nations had long cultural and diplomatic ties. French had been the second language of the Polish aristocracy, and Polish soldiers had served in the armies of Napoleon and the Third Republic. De Gaulle was of no particular mind to safeguard the world from the march of Bolshevism; however, the ideological clash between burgeoning communism and democratic ideals was convenient for his career. Besides, he believed the military mission undertaken by the French to be of much higher moral authority and greater magnitude than those of the other Western powers that chose to support the new Poland.

By the spring of 1919, a contingent of 2,000 French officers had arrived in the Polish capital of Warsaw, and de Gaulle was among them. On April 4, he had signed a contract to remain with the Poles for a period of one year. Assigned to the 5th Chasseurs Polonaise, he endured an arduous trek across Germany by train and began his Polish adventure with the rather mundane role of an instructor. He was also temporarily advanced in rank to major. Stationed at Rembertow, about 12 miles from the heart of Warsaw, his first impression of the soldiers in his charge was that they were undisciplined and lacked military bearing. "Left to themselves these people are good for nothing, and the worst of it is that they believe themselves to excel in everything," he wrote.[2]

Possibly agitated by the general circumstances, he later spouted an ill-advised anti-Semitic slur. "...Utterly loathed by all classes of society and all of them enriched by the war, during which they profited at the expense of the Russians, the Boches and the Poles; and they are quite favorable to a social revolution in which they would gather in a great deal of money in exchange for a few dirty tricks."[3]

No doubt, in later life he was to regret the remark concerning the Jews. However, it must be acknowledged that an undercurrent of anti-Semitism had simmered in Europe for centuries, and de Gaulle had certainly seen evidence of it during his lifetime with the repercussions of the Dreyfus Affair. For better or worse, he had also had time to formulate his own opinions in the matter of Jewish influence on society.

The varied backgrounds and allegiances of the Polish soldiers compounded the difficulty in developing and maintaining unit cohesion, and de Gaulle criticized the generally poor attitude of the troops. To make matters more difficult, he was assigned a Polish orderly who had actually fought for the Germans during the Great War and even directly opposed his regiment at Berry-au-Bac during the heavy fighting of 1915. He was also forced to request a loan from his mother to buy the basic necessities after his quarters were burglarized and he was left with only the clothes on his back.

By August, however, he had recovered sufficient perspective to write to his mother that he was "pretty well as I remember myself before that vile captivity. I have recovered confidence in myself and in the future. The Polish army will have been what I meant it to be, a military restoration for me. Afterwards, I shall work on my own behalf."[4]

While the French had ostensibly come to Poland to assist in establishing an army for defensive purposes, the postwar power vacuum that existed made conditions ripe for a strong leader to seize the initiative, particularly with a force of armed men at his disposal. Such a leader did emerge in the person of Marshal Józef Klemens

Ginet-Pilsudski, himself recently liberated from a German prison camp. Pilsudski had been trained in the Austrian army and now embarked on a mission not only to secure Poland's borders but also to expand them, principally at the expense of the Russians, their long-time enemy to the east.

While his supporters both military and diplomatic looked on with growing concern, Pilsudski moved toward the Baltic and across the Russian frontier into disputed territory. Collectively, the Polish troops advanced more than 100 miles, capturing the great city of Minsk and threatening to move as far eastward as the Dniepr River. In the spring of 1920, the Poles captured Kiev, the capital of the Ukraine, and were approaching the port city of Odessa on the Black Sea. The Baltic states were threatened, and it appeared that an adventurous Pilsudski might know no bounds to his Western-sponsored land grab.

Still shaken by the upheaval of revolution and now apparently nearing a battle for its very existence, Soviet Russia rallied to defend itself, and on April 28, the 27-year-old Marshal Mikhail Tukhachevsky, the fellow prisoner and friend of de Gaulle during World War I, was placed in command. Under Tukhachevsky, the Red Army drove the Poles back to the Vistula River, within striking distance of Warsaw itself. Hurriedly, Poland's benefactors pushed for negotiations to end the war and thus save the country from being overrun.

As these negotiations began, the Russians demanded the installation of a regime that was friendly to their communist ideals, and it appeared that the efforts of the Western powers might have been for nothing. Pilsudski, however, did not sit idly by as the talks commenced. He rapidly organized a counteroffensive to drive the Red Army back from the gates of Warsaw. In a dramatic turn of events that came to be known as the "Miracle of the Vistula," Pilsudski mounted a flank attack and routed the Russians. More than 70,000 prisoners were captured, and Poland was saved.

For his part, following a month's leave with the War Ministry in Paris, de Gaulle had returned to Poland and was given command of an infantry battalion, which he led with distinction during a diversionary attack on the Zbrucz River. His command of the unit was praised, and General Maxime Weygand, a senior French adviser to Pilsudski, was impressed enough to mention Charles in his dispatches, writing of "the particularly brilliant manner in which he accomplished, in the most painful conditions, several missions for the armies in the offensives of August 1920. Demonstrating a sure judgment, exposing himself to direct contact with the enemy in order to get precise intelligence he was, for his chief, a most invaluable support and, for his Polish comrades, the very example of an accomplished officer."[5]

During this time, de Gaulle also took note of two interesting phenomena. He had seen the forceful personality of Pilsudski step up when the opportunity presented itself. The Polish general had assumed the mantle of power during an otherwise chaotic moment in history, and this Pole's assertiveness was impressive. Also, twice he had seen the civilian population of a threatened nation rally to the defense of their country. The Russians had responded against the Poles, and the Poles had energetically mobilized all available resources to stand against the Red Army.

These lessons, undoubtedly, were not lost on Charles de Gaulle two decades later when France was under the heel of the Nazis. Logic dictated that, with a leader to guide them, the French people would also rise to the occasion in their national hour of despair and crisis. In fact, de Gaulle had applied this lesson in his own career, seizing opportunity and determining a personal path to greatness. He had shown strength of character in circumstances that suggested failure and in only a few months emerged from a prison camp to lead men in battle.

When the fighting in Poland subsided, de Gaulle was appointed as aide to General Henri-Albert Niessel, the leader of the French military expedition to the east. De Gaulle wrote an account of his experience in combat, and it was published in the autumn of 1920 in *La Revue de Paris* and titled *The Battle of the Vistula*. He also took some time to enjoy the social life in Warsaw, as best he could.

An austere man never known for indulgences, the young de Gaulle had a weakness for Polish pastries, particularly those served by a small bakery called Chez Blikle. He would consume them at the café, often enjoying the pleasure of his own company, and carry some back to his quarters in a small box tied with string. He was further known to be a frequent guest at the home of Countess Czetwertinska, and light rumors of a romantic liaison between the two wafted through Warsaw. If there were pleasurable diversions during his time in Poland, these few episodes seem to have been the extent of them.

Charles had remained aloof, and other officers were known to have considered him distant. Although he had initially attempted to learn Polish and to deliver his lectures to his students in their native language, this was abandoned in favor of an interpreter who could provide proper diction and pronunciation. He had also taken to wearing white gloves while in uniform, adding to an air of formality and stiffness. Nevertheless, he was known for an ability to keep the attention of an audience and received praise for the content of his presentations. He was further respected for his personal courage, which earned him a Polish decoration for bravery, the Virtuti Militari.

De Gaulle had been mentioned in dispatches at least four times, and other officers had praised him as well, sometimes without being able to resist an appraisal of his personality. One wrote for his personnel file, "An officer of the very first rank; has somewhat lofty airs, however, which may harm him with comrades. A great loss for the infantry instruction school, where it will be exceptionally hard to replace him. Furthermore, the Polish authorities made a most flattering request that he should remain as an instructor in the battalion commander's course."[6]

Another assessment noted, "An officer whose qualities destine him for a very fine military future—a collection of qualities rarely combined in the same degree: a bearing that inspires respect, a strong personality, firm character, active and cool in the presence of danger, wide culture, great intellectual value. Suitable for employment as instructor in military school. Also seems an obvious candidate for the Ecole Supérieure de Guerre."[7]

The Poles had indeed extended an invitation to Charles to lecture at their staff college; however, in January 1921, he was released from his last months of service in Poland and returned to Paris. He could briefly contemplate his future in the peacetime army and consider applying to teach at St. Cyr or possibly for a colonial appointment. His primary reason for returning, though, was to marry his fiancée, Yvonne Vendroux, the daughter of a well-respected family from Calais that owned a biscuit manufacturing company.

They had first met in June 1920, when de Gaulle had been on leave in Paris. Through the contrivances of a matchmaker, Madame Paule Denquin, who happened to be the goddaughter of Henri de Gaulle and a friend of Yvonne's mother, the young officer and the eligible lady had been introduced. It may be surmised that for several months the thought of courtship and marriage had been in the back of Charles's mind. In November 1919, his mother had written to him and discussed the marriage of his brother Xavier.

In a rare moment of sentimentality, Charles had responded, "You know what I hope this year will bring me myself—a family, and, in the peaceful quietness of a deep and sanctified love, the power of giving someone else all the happiness that a man can give."[8]

Madame Denquin supposedly had arranged a chance meeting at the Salon d'Automne, a large exhibition of artwork, during which the two young people began to converse immediately, walking ahead of the friends and other family members gathered and discussing the paintings that hung around them. One version of the courtship recounts that two weeks later Yvonne's brother, Jacques, was involved in a fencing competition and the two families met at a ball at the École Polytechnique on the grounds of the Palace of Versailles. After Charles obtained permission from Jacques, the young couple danced together. Following a few twirls around the floor, the matter was settled and the engagement would soon become official.

Another more fanciful yarn says that de Gaulle had visited a museum with a friend and happened to see a young lady wave to his companion from across a crowded room. Immediately he was said to have asked for an introduction while the orchestra fittingly played the "Destiny Waltz" in the background, and then squeezed himself into a small seat at the Vendroux family table. The lanky officer then allegedly spilled a cup of tea or punch into the lap of the young Yvonne. This incident was supposedly followed by a series of visits to the Vendroux home, first to apologize for the embarrassing spill and then eventually to seal the engagement.

Yet another version says simply enough that Madame Denquin gave a party in October 1920 and invited both families, conspiring with Jacques, who was a willing accomplice, to bring the couple together. They supposedly sat in the drawing room of the house, discussed a popular painting of the time called *La Femme en bleu,* and decided to view the artwork for themselves at the exhibition, where the tea-spilling incident subsequently occurred. A few days later, the Vendroux brother and sister were invited to a ball at St. Cyr, and according to Jacques no dancing took place, although Charles and Yvonne were seen in conversation, seated in separate armchairs and with an appropriate space between them. Then came an official engagement on November 11, and Charles dutifully returned for his final weeks of the posting in Poland.

Although Yvonne had only recently declined the proposal of marriage from another army officer, stating that she had no desire to move from place to place living the life of an army wife, she seemed a match for de Gaulle. He appreciated her quiet dignity, while she seemed to understand him better than others, actually defending his conduct when he lost his temper in front of her entire family over a game of Bridge. Charles was at least 18 inches taller than Yvonne and was ten years her senior. No matter. The two would share their lives with each other for the next half century.[9]

Charles and Yvonne were married on April 7, 1921. They traveled to Lake Maggiore in Italy for their honeymoon, and in December of that year their son, Philippe, was born slightly premature. Two daughters would follow, Elizabeth in 1924, and Anne (born with Down syndrome) in 1928. Soon after their marriage, Charles applied for and was appointed to a teaching position at St. Cyr.

As a professor of history teaching military cadets, this son of a professor was in his element. De Gaulle was assigned a class in nineteenth-century history, particularly teaching the campaigns of Napoleon and boldly castigating the militarism of the emperor, whom he believed had devastated France, leaving the nation "crushed, invaded, drained of blood and of courage, smaller than when he took control, condemned to accept bad frontiers, the evils of which have never been redressed." Later, the content of these lectures would be published in his book *Lettres, Notes et Carnets,* which translates as *Letters, Notes and Notebooks,* and included partially in the 1938 work *La France et Son Armée,* or *France and Her Army.*[10]

One future general at St. Cyr remembered vividly his days as a cadet and that de Gaulle was unequaled as an orator. He wrote years later, "Each one of his lectures was literally an event. He was not the only one to walk into the great amphitheater in boots and with a sword at his side. But with him it all took on a solemn and impressive air. He would take off his kepi, unbuckle his sword which he would put next to his hat on the desk, and then, keeping his gloves on, he would gaze at the audience in a way peculiar to himself. Immensely tall, upright, with his stiff collar tight round his overly long neck, he would talk for two solid hours without looking at his notes. He quite overcame us. He made such an impression on his audiences that presently the cadres of the school came and sat on the front benches, field officers and then generals!

"The culminating point of these lectures—there were a dozen altogether—was when, dealing with the fighting men of Verdun, he paused at length, then roared 'Gentlemen, stand up!' and you would see the generals present rise just as we did, the ordinary students, while he paid homage to those who died at Douaumont. This tells one something about the captain's extraordinary ascendancy over men of all ages and ranks."[11]

During one lecture, de Gaulle foreshadowed the circumstances that would compel him to flee France and turn against the Vichy government in 1940. "History does not teach fatalism," he told an assembly. "There are moments when the will of a handful of free men breaks through determinism and opens up new roads. People get the history they deserve. When you lament a misfortune and fear that worse is to come people will tell you, 'It is the law of history. It is the will of evolution.' They will explain it all very lucidly. Stand up, gentlemen, against such clever cowardice. It is worse than stupidity. It is the sin against the Holy Spirit."[12]

Charles de Gaulle was firmly convinced that men made history, and not the other way around. It was the sacred duty of Frenchmen to uphold and affirm the honor of their country during its darkest days. At St. Cyr, de Gaulle found his voice and the stage presence which would serve him so well in the years to come. Once again, he also felt the stirrings of greatness.

Whether or not it was the result of the intervention of fate, the young couple had hit upon a stroke of luck, or Charles engineered the situation, the de Gaulles located a small apartment on the Boulevard de Grenelle in Paris, near the home of none other than Marshal Pétain, the hero of Verdun. Pétain, a notorious womanizer, had married a previously divorced woman who was shunned in many social circles. It made the renewal of the friendship between the marshal and the captain somewhat awkward, but the two admired each other greatly, and the commander of the École Supérieure de Guerre, the prestigious national war college, had been a subordinate and follower of Pétain during the war.

For those officers who aspired to senior positions within the French army, completion of the École Supérieure was virtually a prerequisite. De Gaulle taught at St. Cyr for only a year and began to plan his entry into the school. Since he had not held a position on the general staff, he was not guaranteed a place at the École Supérieure, which had been closed during the war. There was also a long list of officers seeking appointments—officers with impressive combat records who had not been sidelined by capture.

Nevertheless, he gained entry to the college through his high score on a competitive examination. On May 2, 1922, his name appeared on the list of 129 officers of the 44th Promotion to the École Supérieure. Based on his examination score and other criteria, he ranked in the top one-third of his class at the beginning of the two-year course of study.

Since his days as a prisoner of war, de Gaulle had been aware of a new weapon, the tank, which had first seen combat in the autumn of 1917. He had read of its appearance on the battlefield in German newspapers and become intrigued by its firepower and mobility. He had also seen a few armored vehicles in Poland, and in a report to the general staff of his experience in the East, he advised, "Tanks should be brought into the field as a body, and not separately."[13] It was perhaps the first glimpse of his appreciation for the role the tank would play a generation later during World War II.

Through his combat experience, de Gaulle had also gained an appreciation of the lethality of modern weapons such as the machine gun and heavy artillery and their potential for the support of mobile warfare. While some military theorists had begun to develop tactical doctrine surrounding the offensive use of the tank, most senior officers in the French army had become convinced by the carnage of the Great War that strong fixed fortifications, a heavy defensive line that was deemed impregnable, would be pre-eminent in the wars of the future. His developing theories on modern warfare would increasingly place him at odds with the postwar military establishment.

When de Gaulle entered the École Supérieure in November 1922, he was already something of a marked man. His experience in World War I and Poland notwithstanding, he was widely known as the protégé of Pétain, and this was both a great asset and a hindrance. His intellectual prowess and his detached personality were potentially a volatile combination as well. In short, it might have been easy for those at the military college to dislike Charles de Gaulle without knowing him—and sometimes knowing him made the exercise even less of a stretch. While his haughtiness was at times intolerable, his conceit unbearable, he remained *le poulain préféré*, the preferred chicken, of Pétain.

From the outset, de Gaulle had difficulty playing the role of pupil, particularly since it was obvious to him that his experience in both the field and the classroom surpassed that of some of his professors. De Gaulle habitually corrected the errors of his instructors and challenged their thinking—particularly when it came to the discussion of static defense that appeared to endorse the trench warfare of World War I as the prevailing doctrine during wars to come. The 33-year-old captain knew the tank would play a principal role in the future of land warfare, and he was determined to stand his ground, even if it proved to be to his own detriment.

In spite of his aloof personality, de Gaulle did make a favorable impression on some of his classmates. One fellow student remembered resting under a large oak tree following a strenuous exercise in which the two had been partnered. As they relaxed and smoked cigarettes, he commented, "My friend, I must tell you something which will no doubt make you smile. I have a curious feeling that you are pledged to a great destiny." Rather than laughing the comment away, de Gaulle thoughtfully replied, "Yes. I think so too."[14]

During his two years at the École Supérieure, de Gaulle could not control his growing disdain for the rigidity of the curriculum and the officer corps that espoused it. While he had no experience with tanks in combat, he had seen the advantages of rapid movement on the battlefield during his service in Poland. Fueled by the fact that he considered virtually all of those around him to be intellectually inferior, he antagonized and provoked at nearly every opportunity.

Further alienating himself from the officers at the École Supérieure, he published his first book, *La Discorde chez l'Ennemi,* in the summer of 1924, prior to graduating. While describing the problems facing the German government and armed forces during World War I, the book also put forth numerous ideas that were opposed to those being taught at the school. The very idea that a junior officer had been presumptuous enough to publish such a book was infuriating to the senior officers.

Published by a former fellow prisoner of war, de Gaulle's book sold fewer than 1,000 copies. However, his determination to see the project through was evidence of his willingness to pursue his own agenda despite the potential interpersonal difficulties that might later result from such conduct. His insight, too, was often stunning.

He described the preoccupation of the German people with "the Superman with his exceptional character, the will to power, the taste for risk...appeared to these passionate and vicious men as the ideal they ought to attain; they freely opted to belong to this formidable Nietzschean elite which, while pursuing its own glory, is convinced that it is serving the general interest which constrains the mass of slaves while contemptuous of it, and which does not stop before human suffering except to salute it as necessary and as desirable."

During his second year, Colonel Moyrand, an instructor in field tactics, noted that de Gaulle was "a very intelligent officer, cultivated and serious, greatly gifted. Unfortunately spoils his incontestable qualities by his excessive assurance, his severity toward the opinions of others and his attitude of being a king in exile. Moreover, he appears to have more aptitude for general studies and for the synthesis of a problem than for its detailed examination and the practicalities of its execution."[15]

It was with this instructor that the most notable example of de Gaulle's lack of respect for authority occurred in the summer of 1924. During field exercises conducted in the vicinity of the village of Bar-sur-Aube, near Paris, Moyrand placed de Gaulle in command of an army corps and challenged him to make appropriate decisions during a rapidly changing engagement. The captain discharged his duties calmly, achieved the desired results, and was declared the winner of the mock battle.

In the process, however, de Gaulle's arrogance had continued to get the better of him. Moyrand, no doubt already well acquainted with his pupil's attitude, assembled the officers who had taken part in the exercise and attempted to put de Gaulle on the spot with a series of pointed questions. As de Gaulle responded to each of these with apparent indifference and Moyrand became increasingly frustrated, the tension within the room continued to grow. Finally, Moyrand posed a seemingly irrelevant question concerning the location of supplies for one of the regiments on the right flank of de Gaulle's command. De Gaulle turned to his chief of staff, Captain Chateauvieux, seated beside him, and directed the other officer to answer Moyrand's question.

"But I asked you the question, de Gaulle," Moyrand blurted. With the door wide open, de Gaulle strode through, calmly responding, "Colonel, you entrusted me with the responsibilities of an army corps command. If I had to assume those of my subordinates as well, I should not have my mind free to fulfill my assignment satisfactorily." He quickly followed with the Latin phrase "*de minimis non curat praetor*" (the law does not concern itself with small matters), and directed Chateauvieux once again to answer the question.

A seething Moyrand then stated the obvious. "We knew you considered many tasks beneath you. Very well. I am now clear in my mind about you."[16] De Gaulle considered the encounter of little consequence, other than to validate his intellectual superiority and his right to assert it.

For graduates of the École Supérieure, three critical ratings could well determine their level of success during the remainder of their careers. Very good, good, or average grades were meted out according to the findings of the instructors. It was well understood that only those who were determined to be of the highest caliber could have any assurance of appointment to a prominent position in the army and aspire to the highest echelon of command. Others were relegated to dead-end positions in unglamorous locations with bleak prospects for their future in the military.

De Gaulle was certain that his performance would merit the highest level; however, when the time came to assess the upstart captain's proficiency a controversy ensued. Several instructors wanted to put de Gaulle in his place, with a mediocre rating. This would send a loud and clear message to the impudent officer and assure that his future in the army was virtually without promise. Other instructors wanted to go even further and rate de Gaulle in the lowest-performing group.

However, the commander of the school, General Dufieux, stepped in to quiet some of the heated discussion. More important, Pétain had gotten wind of the furor surrounding de Gaulle's rating. Further, he decided to investigate the embarrassing controversy surrounding the exchange between de Gaulle and Moyrand during the field exercise.

Pétain assessed de Gaulle's conduct during the exercise, went as far as to conduct private discussions with both antagonists, and determined that de Gaulle had discharged his duties properly. He insisted that his protégé's record be reviewed and considered more fairly. Nevertheless, Dufieux could not give in to the marshal's wishes entirely. To do so would have thoroughly undermined his credibility with the cadre of the École Supérieure. Thus, a final rating of "good" was issued.

During an assembly of the officer-students, the names of the graduates were read aloud along with their final standing. For de Gaulle, it was a supreme humiliation and miscarriage of justice. His reaction was predictable. He erupted in a tirade against the leaders of the school and vowed, "I will come back to this dirty hole only when I am commandant of it. Then you will see how things will change."[17] He would have his opportunity for redress, facilitated by Pétain, but that would come later.

CHAPTER 4

Restless Recalcitrant

FOLLOWING HIS INAUSPICIOUS GRADUATION FROM THE ÉCOLE SUPÉRIEURE, Charles de Gaulle was required to swallow the bitter pill of an assignment that could hardly have been more obscure, relegated to the backwater supply department of the army of occupation in Germany. In October 1924, he was placed in the Fourth Bureau of the occupation army, sent to the city of Mainz in the Rhineland, and given responsibility for the refrigeration, supply, and storage of food.

Having once even entertained the possibility of becoming a lecturer at the École Supérieure, he was now depressed to the point that he considered leaving the army. His first book had been published, and he might well become an educator at a civilian university. Yet he took advantage of the free time and the location of his posting to make a further assessment of the character of the German people, refining his command of their language and reinforcing his somewhat prophetic stance that another war with Germany loomed in the future.

Prior to his departure for Mainz, de Gaulle had visited Pétain, who undoubtedly considered the entire affair at the École Supérieure a personal insult. His own reputation and standing among the senior officers of the French army had been somewhat tarnished by the series of events. Therefore, within nine months of his posting to the equivalent of career oblivion, de Gaulle was under consideration to return to Paris and join Pétain's personal staff.

The marshal now held the posts of vice president of the Superior Council of War and Inspector General of the army. He had become concerned that the postwar socialist government, burdened by overwhelming debt, might curtail military expenditures and even shorten the length of conscription for the common soldier from three years to as brief a term as one year. In response to such a threat, Pétain intended to produce a history of the armed forces of France and their role in protecting and preserving the state.

He had also begun to write a book that amounted to a perspective on the French soldier with particular attention to the army's role in the Great War, and this foundation could easily be included in a more comprehensive work. A logical choice to participate in the literary effort was none other than de Gaulle, a gifted writer who had committed to memory most—if not all—of the famous names, dates and engagements in French military history.

By October 1925, de Gaulle was working with a group of staff officers under the direction of Colonel Laure, Pétain's private secretary, and Colonel Duchene, the marshal's chief of staff. Pétain imposed strict guidelines on the authors, and it was readily apparent that they were serving as ghostwriters for their senior commander. Despite a lack of freedom to compose in his own, more flowing style of prose, these were happy times for de Gaulle, and his research and writing resulted in several chapters of the book.

Pétain's secretary remembered the sight of an enthusiastic de Gaulle reporting for work. "He wore a bowler hat and he carried a stick, and he always looked preoccupied," she related. "As he walked he looked up into the sky and waved his stick as though he were writing in the air. The marshal was very hard to please; he often used to cross out and correct. But I remember Captain de Gaulle's pieces very well. They were always perfectly legible, and the marshal made few corrections."[1]

In Paris, de Gaulle was allowed to work in an office by himself, while other writers had to share space. Perhaps this was an acknowledgment by Pétain that his protégé was the most talented officer in the French army when it came to placing thoughts on paper. In the midst of the current project, de Gaulle was taken aside by Pétain and asked to produce a brief treatise on the importance of fixed fortifications in the past, present, and future defense of France.

The irony is readily apparent, with de Gaulle, an advocate of firepower and mobility, promoting immovable, static fortresses garrisoned by troops obliged to occupy defensive positions that could not facilitate offensive action. But he complied with orders, and within weeks, the article was finished. It appeared in *French Military Review* in December 1925 with the title "Role Historique des Places Francaises" (The Historical Role of French Fortifications) and was received enthusiastically, particularly because it appeared to reinforce the prevailing defensive attitude of the French military establishment. Later the article was utilized to bolster the argument for the construction of the Maginot Line, which remains a monument to the failure of the French army to defend its homeland against the Nazis in 1940.

De Gaulle, however, had not sold out to the predominant school of thought. His work does acknowledge the merits of fixed fortifications for defensive purposes but stops short of pronouncing them the savior of France in armed conflict. They could provide a degree of security, but more important, they would serve as bases for maneuver, for offensive action, for the counterthrust against an aggressive enemy.

A friend of de Gaulle, Captain Lucien Nachin, who had served with him in the 33rd Infantry Regiment and who would later write a 1944 biography of de Gaulle, observed, "This article carried public opinion with it and the plan for the fortification of the northeastern frontier was completely successful. Perhaps too successful. Indeed, was it not reasonable to be uneasy at the excessive confidence that this armored protection, said to be impregnable, would arouse in the country?"[2]

De Gaulle, concerned that some of his conclusions were misinterpreted, responded, "In my humble opinion the defensive organization must not be—as many wish—part of the operational plan. The necessary and permanent defensive organization, which is related to the geographical, political and even state of morale in which the country finds itself, is a question for the government. The operational plan is a question for the command. The latter takes account of the strongholds (whatever their form) in its projects, as one of its means, exactly as it takes account of its forces, of the materiel and of economic power."[3]

Undoubtedly, there was one other reason for Pétain to bring de Gaulle back to Paris. For the marshal, the indignity visited upon de Gaulle at the École Supérieure was reminiscent of his own perceived injustice at the hands of generals who were out of touch with the modern realities of war. In 1900 he had been relieved from the post of instructor at the National Firing School because he had taught tactics that were not endorsed at the time. Later, as an instructor of infantry tactics at the École Supérieure, he had made enemies while stressing the importance of firepower over the heroism of the infantry charge. In the killing fields of World War I, his assertion was proven correct. Now, as the hero of Verdun, he would leverage de Gaulle's unfortunate experience and provide an opportunity for his protégé to square the ledger while having his own retribution in the process.

The forum for the drama of sweet revenge was to be a series of three lectures, delivered by de Gaulle, presided over by Pétain, and featuring the compulsory attendance of all instructors and students at the École Supérieure de Guerre. Pétain contacted the commander, General Pierre Hering, who was coincidentally one of the marshal's most devoted followers and would remain so to the end, and advised him of the situation, explaining de Gaulle's shabby treatment. Hering was pleased to accommodate the marshal's request.

The first lecture was scheduled for April 27, 1927, four months after de Gaulle's name appeared on a list of officers to be promoted to the rank of major. He had languished as a captain for nearly 11 years, evidence in itself of the vindictive nature of the French army's senior officers of the time and to the fact that de Gaulle had, in large part, reaped the fruit of the seeds he had sown.

On the evening of the first lecture, a throng of officers made way for Pétain to enter. The marshal, theatrically enough, paused to allow de Gaulle to enter before him with the comment, "The honor is yours. It is the lecturer's privilege to lead the way. After entering he is entitled to teach what he wishes. That is how I applied it to myself, expressing ideas different from those of my time."[4]

Following a brief introduction by Pétain, de Gaulle took the stage and spoke on the topic of military leadership, weaving in a lengthy tribute to the life and service of his benefactor. Immaculately dressed, he placed his kepi to the side, removed his sword, and then proceeded to take off his trademark white gloves. Not yet confirmed as a major, he wore the braid of a captain in an amphitheater filled with officers who outranked him. The fact that de Gaulle was an immensely talented speaker was not enough to assuage the uneasiness of those who listened. The message was clear, both that of the subject matter and of the unprecedented lecture series by a junior officer, whose sponsor was a marshal of France.

On the first evening, his topic was "Action in War and the Leader." He commented to the assembly, "Powerful personalities, organized for conflict, crises, and great events, do not always possess the easy manners and superficially attractive qualities which are well accepted in everyday life. They are usually blunt and uncompromising, without social graces. Although deep down the masses may obscurely do them justice, acknowledging their superiority, they are rarely loved and in consequence rarely find an easy way to the top. Selection boards are inclined to deal more in personal charm than merit."[5] During the successive lectures, de Gaulle quoted numerous statesmen, soldiers, philosophers, and scientists.

The veiled reference to his own treatment was irrefutable. Although he maintained an external air of dignity, he most certainly was euphoric during the delivery of the barb to a captive audience. For many of those who had been instructors two years before and now listened to their former student, the series of lectures was never forgotten, and the already festering bitterness would last a lifetime. De Gaulle's long-awaited vindication had come at a price.

The lecture on military leadership was followed by others on the topics of character and prestige. Together, with minor editing and modification, these were published in *French Military Review* in 1930 and 1931. Combined with additional chapters, they comprised the majority of his book *Le Fil de l'Épée,* or *The Edge of the Sword,* which was published in 1932.

De Gaulle worked to perfect *Le Fil de l'Épée* for nearly a decade after its publication and until the eve of World War II. Often quoted, its most famous passage remains one of the artist's finest self-portraits.

In action, no more criticism! Wishes and hopes turn toward the leader as iron toward the magnet. When the crisis comes, it is he who is followed, it is he who raises the burden with his own arms, though they may break in doing so, and carries it on his shoulders though they may crack under it. The ordinary run of events is not favorable to him with regard to his superiors. He is confident of his judgment and aware of his strength, and he never sacrifices anything to the desire to please. He is often far removed from passive obedience by the fact that he derives his firmness and power of decision from himself and by no means from any order. He desires that he should be allotted a task and left to carry it out by himself, a requirement found unbearable by many leaders who, for want of seeing things as a whole, take great care of details and nourish themselves on formalities. "Vain and undisciplined" say the mediocre minds, treating the soft mouthed thoroughbred as though it were an ass that will not go forward, they being totally unaware of the fact that asperity is the failing of powerful characters, that support is to be gained only from that which stands firm, and that strong, unaccommodating hearts are preferable to easygoing, yielding minds. But as soon as matters grow serious and the danger urgent, as soon as the general safety requires immediate initiative, a taste for risk, and firmness, the whole viewpoint changes and justice comes into its own. A kind of tidal wave sweeps the man of character to the forefront.[6]

De Gaulle believed that disobedience and refusal to conform, when called for, were both necessary and noble. During his second lecture, he noted that Admiral John Jellicoe of the British Royal Navy had failed to pursue the German High Seas Fleet following the Battle of Jutland in 1916. Admiral John Fisher, First Sea Lord, assessed Jellicoe's performance at Jutland in comparison to Horatio Nelson, the hero of Trafalgar, commenting that Jellicoe "has all of Nelson's qualities but one: He does not know how to disobey."[7]

For all his effort, de Gaulle had not captivated the audience at the École Supérieure. Much of his commentary may either have been more than his listeners could comprehend or cared to listen to considering the source. De Gaulle had held true to form, delivering his lectures during three consecutive weeks. When he had finished, his audience had reached the pinnacle of resentment. Needless to say, General Hering was the recipient of numerous complaints following the series, which was repeated for a civilian audience at the Sorbonne in Paris some time later. The response of the general public was tepid.

Nevertheless, with the patronage of Marshal Pétain, the career of Charles de Gaulle had been revived, perhaps a more apt description of the process than the term "rehabilitated," which has also been used by historians. Despite his difficulties and the grateful acknowledgment that it was Pétain who made his future in the French army something of substance once again, de Gaulle would likely not have accepted the notion that he had been the subject of rehabilitation. Those to whom he lectured were the ones in need of such measures. It was they whose minds were closed to the inevitability of change.

Although the reputation of Pétain would be tarnished during and after the Vichy years, he did contribute mightily to the Allied victory in World War I, the preservation of the French army during the interwar years, and the resurrection of the career of his protégé. He recognized de Gaulle's brilliance and foresight and had been willing to stake his own honor and prestige, at least in part, in an effort to raise de Gaulle to prominence and position him to play some meaningful role in the future of France.

The dedication of *Le Fil de l'Épée* reads appropriately, "This work could only be dedicated to you, *Monsieur le Maréchal,* since nothing demonstrates better than your glory what virtue can be brought to action through the illumination of pure thought." The first copy of the book was sent by the author to his patron with the inscription, "Homage from C. de Gaulle in deepest respect and devotion."

Years later, with Pétain disgraced after World War II and his death sentence commuted by de Gaulle to life in prison, it was said that this copy of *Le Fil de l'Épée* was among the personal possessions the marshal carried with him to exile on l'Île d'Yeu, a windswept island off the west coast of French Brittany, where he would die in 1951 at the age of 95.

By the autumn of 1927, de Gaulle's promotion to major had finally been confirmed, and he departed from Pétain's staff with the historical work, tentatively titled *Le Soldat,* or *The Soldier,* which he had originally come to Paris to complete, remaining unfinished.

Apparently, Pétain had moved on to other, more pressing concerns. The next posting for Charles was as commander of the 19th Battalion of Light Infantry, a unit of the Alpine Chasseurs. It was his first command of troops in more than a decade and required him to return to Germany and the city of Trier.

The new commander approached his charge with characteristic zeal. He immediately set about imprinting his own style on the battalion, wearing his beret tipped to the right rather than the left as it had been traditionally worn. His subordinate officers and other ranks complied, and when his superior officer objected de Gaulle simply ignored the inquiry since there was no specific regulation that prohibited the change. Although the beret incident seems minor, it is evidence of de Gaulle's intent to disobey. His men, however, gained admiration for him and quickly began to call him an "honored chausseur."

The battalion was supposed to be an elite formation, and de Gaulle drove his men relentlessly. Hours of drill, long marches in difficult terrain and inclement weather, and continuous work to improve marksmanship kept the soldiers razor sharp; however, a pair of notable incidents prompted some to request transfers from the unit and precipitated an investigation.

The 19th Battalion had previously taken part in a field exercise in the autumn of 1928, and with the onset of winter de Gaulle was determined to execute another such round of training. This exercise would involve a crossing of the Moselle River, now covered in ice. With preparations finalized for the venture, the battalion received an order to cancel the troop movement, and although de Gaulle was angered by the directive he complied. The battalion had already moved to a camp near the town of Bitche several days earlier and would be required to march back to Trier.

As the return trek commenced, de Gaulle decided that he would complete it during the night rather than resting his men along the way and finishing in daylight. Instead of informing his subordinates at the time, he gave the command of the battalion to another officer and, accompanied by a pair of bicyclists, rode ahead to a crossroads. About an hour later, when the formation had reached the crossroads as well, he told the other officers of his decision. When they protested that arrangements had been made to camp that night and that permission to conduct a forced march and enter an occupied town at a late hour would require the approval of the commanding general, he brushed aside their concerns and curtly replied that he would accept full responsibility.

The ill-advised forced march had come just with the onset of a serious influenza epidemic that gripped the French army in Germany, causing the serious illnesses and deaths of a number of soldiers. Concerned with an alarming number of transfer requests, the commander had previously threatened any soldier who petitioned for reassignment from the 19th Battalion with imprisonment. One soldier apparently pushed too far, asking his representative in parliament to facilitate a transfer with the defense ministry. De Gaulle kept his word and had the soldier jailed for two weeks.

Indeed, there were protests, not only from the soldier and the parliamentarian, but also from the people of Trier, whose peace had been disturbed by the nocturnal return of the 19th Battalion. Coupled with news of the raging influenza epidemic that was reported to have hit de Gaulle's command particularly hard, the protests reached the Minister of War, Paul Panlevé, and resulted in an official inquiry. De Gaulle faced 60 days in prison and potentially an ignominious end to his military career. However, he remained strong in the knowledge that he still enjoyed the favor of Marshal Pétain. Those who warned of harsh punishment were confidently told, "I belong to the house of Pétain. Everything will die down."[8]

De Gaulle was ordered to present himself before the commander of the army of occupation in Germany, but prior to the scheduled date he traveled by train to Paris to explain his actions to the marshal. Pétain quashed the investigation with a telephone call to his friend

Panlevé. Fortunately, everyone involved was able to save face, since the soldier in question had requested his transfer two days before the issuing of de Gaulle's order forbidding such actions. One member of the commission that visited Trier to report on the condition of the men of the 19th Battalion praised de Gaulle for personally going into mourning upon the death of a soldier who had no family of his own and stated, "There have been a large number of deaths in the 19th Battalion of Light Infantry, but these are certainly not due to the way in which the men have been treated. This battalion is admirably commanded."[9]

De Gaulle was not required to appear before the commander of the army of occupation and received no punishment for the incident. To those who knew of the circumstances, though, it appeared that he lived by and benefited from a double standard. He acted swiftly in response to those under his command who chose to disobey orders or act in a manner contradictory to his direction. However, when he did the same he was quick to run to Pétain for protection.

Combined with de Gaulle's characteristically high opinion of himself, the incident served to make the outspoken officer all the more detestable to some. One subordinate officer summed up the feeling that was shared by a number of military men, saying that de Gaulle stood out not so much because of his great height but due to the fact that his ego shone like a beacon from afar.

This action on de Gaulle's behalf proved to be one of the final favors Pétain would bestow on the brilliant young officer. The marshal had grown tired of bailing out the arrogant de Gaulle and believed he had taken advantage of his position too often. In fact, the relationship between the two men appears to have begun to erode earlier in the year. At the center of the disagreement was the original manuscript that had been shelved by Pétain.

While de Gaulle was in Germany, Pétain once again became interested, if only in passing, in the progress of the manuscript tentatively titled *Le Soldat*. Early in 1928, de Gaulle received a letter from another officer, a Colonel Audet, who had been selected by Pétain to work as a writer. The letter related that Pétain had asked the officer to pick up where de Gaulle had left off. It is difficult to believe that de Gaulle had initially labored under any delusion that his role in the project was anything more than that of a ghostwriter and that he would receive anything more than a passing acknowledgment for contributing to a work that would be published under Pétain's illustrious name. However, he reacted as though shocked by the letter from Audet.

"I am touched by the frank and open confidence that you show me, and I thank you for it," Charles responded.

> You already know my opinion. A book is a man. Until now that man has been myself. If some other person, even if he were a Monstesquieu, even if he were you yourself colonel, takes a hand in it then one or two things must come about—either he writes a different book or he destroys mine, which will no longer have any character and will therefore be worthless. If the marshal wishes you to write another book, I have no sort of objection to offer. I shall purely and simply take my book back. But if it is a question of mangling my ideas, my philosophy and my style I do object and I am going to tell the marshal so. The marshal has never been willing to acknowledge the difference that exists between a book and a piece of writing for the general staff. That is why I have often thought that this business would end badly.[10]

The divergent interpretations of the role each was to play in producing *Le Soldat* are evident. Pétain believed that de Gaulle was writing under his patronage and direction with the understanding that his function was essentially that of a ghostwriter. De Gaulle, on the other hand, had begun to feel strongly that the book was his creation and that he, therefore, deserved the lion's share of the credit for its production. While de Gaulle refers to *Le Soldat* as his own, he was more correctly involved with a group of writers and assigned a section of the book, primarily dealing with French strategy and tactics during World War I.

Pétain, in his editorial capacity, may well have found de Gaulle's assessment of French performance during the Great War detrimental not only to his conduct of some operations but also to his doctrine of fixed firepower as evidenced by the previous writings, which formed the basis for advocating the construction of the Maginot Line. As it turned out, the *Le Soldat* was never published as a completed work. However, de Gaulle would use seven of the ten chapters he penned as the basis for his book *La France et Son Armée,* which was published in 1938.

Aside from the difficulties with Pétain, de Gaulle was particularly challenged during 1928 by personal tragedy. In December, his third child, Anne, was born with Down syndrome. She was to live 20 years, and although her condition was the source of great sorrow for her parents it was also the source of great tenderness on the part of de Gaulle. Such displays of pure emotion were rare for de Gaulle. On more than one occasion, he remarked that Anne had not asked to come into the world and that the family would do all that it could to make her happy.

Professionally, Major de Gaulle neared the end of his two-year term as commander of the 19th Battalion in the autumn of 1929. The French army of the Rhine was reorganized, and his command was to be disbanded. De Gaulle requested a posting to the Middle East. Such an assignment would at least temporarily defuse the disagreement with Pétain, and in fact Pétain encouraged de Gaulle to seek a tour of duty in the Middle East in order to advance his career during peacetime.

Regardless, de Gaulle's towering ego undoubtedly contributed to his desire for a venture beyond the European continent. He had come to believe that Pétain was merely using his talents as a writer much in the same way that de Gaulle had utilized Pétain's patronage to salvage his own career in the military. In contrast, bending to Pétain's wishes in regard to *Le Soldat,* quietly and dutifully ghostwriting as he had been asked, was a small price to pay for the enormous benefits the marshal's favor had afforded him. Each had stretched his usefulness to the other beyond the limits of goodwill and the endurance of such forceful personalities.

On October 30, 1929, the entire de Gaulle family sailed to Beirut, Lebanon, where Charles assumed the duties of chief of operations and intelligence for the French army of the Levant. Before his departure, he had written prophetically to a friend of his impression of future relations with Germany.

"The French Army of Occupation on the Rhine will not be there much longer," he commented. "The force of circumstances is knocking down what remains of Europe's vital, fixed frontiers. One should realize that the Anschluss [the union of Germany and Austria that occurred in 1938] is close at hand and that Germany will soon take back, peacefully or by force, the territory seized from her for the benefit of Poland. After that, they will ask us to return Alsace. That seems to me to be written in the stars."[11]

Utilizing much of his time in the Middle East to travel and gain insight into the nature of France's far-flung colonial empire, Charles became increasingly convinced that the manpower and treasure required to maintain such an empire were more than the nation should invest. He wrote, "We are scarcely having any impact. . . . Nothing has ever been achieved in this part of the world without firmness. As I see it, our destiny must be either to make a real impression or to leave."[12]

Ironically, his experience in the Middle East would influence his French nationalism decades later during his term as president of the Fifth Republic. His decision to grant independence to a number of France's colonial possessions may well have been influenced by his impressions while traveling around the territories of the French mandate during the 1930s.

Although he had hoped for a position as a lecturer at the École Supérieure de Guerre when he returned from the Middle East in late

1931, Charles was instead appointed, with the recommendation of Pétain, to the Secretariat-General of the Supreme Council of Defense, which the old marshal had founded in 1922 to maintain French military preparedness. Pétain, now in his midseventies, had retired, and his successor as commander of the French army was General Maxime Weygand, under whom de Gaulle had served in Poland.

After writing a history of the French troops in the Middle East, Charles was charged with an overview of mobilization and the utilization of resources in the event of another war, updating a survey that had been completed as early as 1923 but received little attention from a succession of impotent governments during the next five years. The report itself did not reach the French legislative body for more than a year after de Gaulle's revisions, and its final version was not approved until the spring of 1938.

Meanwhile, in the midst of the Great Depression, France had committed millions of francs to the construction of the Maginot Line in 1934. Although the construction of the string of defensive fortifications was costly, it was deemed the least expensive alternative for defense against invasion from the east for the cash-strapped French government, and it also conformed to the standard doctrine of the army. Hitler and the Nazis had risen to power in Germany, and the *Anschluss* with Austria had indeed taken place. In the autumn of 1938, Great Britain and France would seal the fate of Czechoslovakia by signing the infamous Munich Pact with the Nazis. Within a year, France would be at war once again.

The five years that de Gaulle spent with the Supreme Council were valuable in that he became thoroughly acquainted with the interaction of political and military factions within the highest levels of the French government. He had also become aware of the logistical challenges of mobilizing and coordinating large numbers of troops. Although the retired Pétain maintained a degree of influence, Charles de Gaulle, promoted to lieutenant colonel on December 25, 1933, now felt further empowered to expound on tactical theories with which he had become familiar and that might even place him further at odds with his mentor. Ideas began to crystallize.

"From 1932 to 1937, under 14 governments," he wrote in his war memoirs,

> I found myself involved in a planning capacity in the whole range of political, technical and administrative activity concerning the country's defense. The work I had to do, the discussions at which I was present, the contacts I was obliged to make, showed me the extent of our resources but also the feebleness of the state. For the disjointedness of government was rife all over this field. Not—certainly—that the men who figured there lacked intelligence or patriotism; on the contrary I saw men of incontestable value and sometimes of great talent come to the head of the ministries. But the political game consumed them and paralyzed them.[13]

For his part, Charles de Gaulle appeared more determined than ever to rise above the politics of the times, assume a firm stand, assert his own correctness, and deal with or disdain the fallout that ensued as he saw fit. Even during his lifetime, a Gaullist cult of personality would begin to grow around France's hero of World War II. Among other accomplishments or details of his career that may well have been embellished by his ardent followers, de Gaulle is quite probably given more credit that he actually deserves in developing a doctrine of mobile warfare and the employment of armored fighting vehicles on the battlefield. Nevertheless, he was an advocate of both and did what he could to modernize French military thinking.

De Gaulle was undoubtedly aware that the tank had made its combat debut during World War I. He had attended the refresher course on the technological developments which had taken place while he was a prisoner of war. He had spent a brief time with a motorized army unit based at Satory in 1921. He had read the works of British Major General J. F. C. Fuller and Captain B. H. Liddell Hart, which had appeared as early as 1920. He knew of proposals made to the French military establishment during the preceding decade by General Jean-Baptiste Estienne and General Joseph Doumenc that advocated the formation of armored divisions. He was also keenly aware that these proposals had been shunted aside.

Estienne had actually said to a gathering several years earlier, "Think gentlemen of the formidable advantages, both strategic and tactical, which would accrue to the heaviest armies of the past few years: 100,000 men capable of covering 50 miles in a single night.... Imagine breakthrough tanks of 50 to 100 tons... crushing all obstacles, disemboweling houses with armored infantry and accompanying artillery. Soon the first enemy lines are crushed and the light tanks rush forward, as the cavalry once did, to seal the victory."[14]

Still, the French military mind-set in the interwar years was purely defensive, dependent upon big guns housed in massive fortresses. The Maginot Line, however, did not fully extend across the northeastern frontier of France. Debate had raged in the national assembly as to the merits of extending the line from the Swiss frontier to the English Channel. Finally, it was decided that the cost of such a venture would not only be prohibitive but also would antagonize the government of neighboring Belgium, with which relations had been strained for some time. Besides, the Belgians had constructed some fortifications of their own.

Therefore, the construction of the Maginot Line was limited primarily to the disputed border provinces of Alsace and Lorraine and extended northward along the boundary with Luxembourg to the edge of the Ardennes Forest, which was considered impenetrable by a military force of any consequence. The Maginot Line was not only flawed in theory as a defensive bulwark against the Germans but also inherently weakened by its open flank in the north. When the Germans executed their invasion of France and the Low Countries on May 10, 1940, they chose not to attack the Maginot Line directly. Instead, they subdued Belgian fortifications with precision assaults by glider-borne infantry while their mechanized units outflanked the Maginot Line through the Ardennes. De Gaulle was among the few military men in France during the 1930s who refused to accept the Maginot Line as a guarantee of French security.

While working with the Supreme Council during the mid-1930s, de Gaulle had read an article by his friend Captain Nachin, which discussed the employment of tanks with the French army. Through Nachin, he had also been introduced to Colonel Émile Mayer, who was more than 80 years old but still a visionary. Mayer hosted a weekly gathering of officers to discuss relevant topics of the day at a café on the Boulevard Montparnasse near the War Ministry, and de Gaulle began to attend these meetings.

During one of these meetings, de Gaulle embarked upon a discussion of Nachin's article and began to relate to Mayer his own vision of a highly trained, mobile army of 100,000 professional soldiers, similar in concept to that of Estienne. The idea was a radical departure from France's tradition of the "Levée en Masse," the conscription of thousands of civilian-soldiers, which dated to the time of Napoleon. Further, de Gaulle began to elaborate on his expanding concepts of the tank and motorized infantry in warfare. It was Mayer who supposedly encouraged Charles to prepare an article concerning his theories for publication in a military magazine.

De Gaulle set to work, and on May 10, 1933, the article appeared in *La Revue politique et parlementaire* (*Political and Parliamentary Review*). Its title was *Vers l'Armée de Métier* (*Toward a Professional Army*).

Published with the same title almost a year to the day later, the book that followed was a thin volume of just over 45,000 words. Neither the article nor the book created much fanfare. Although it was later translated into English under the title *The Army of the Future,* it sold only about 750 copies in France. De Gaulle was probably well aware that his treatise would receive only passing attention. However, he nevertheless felt it his duty to sound the alarm, to identify the danger that loomed with a continuation of outmoded military thinking, and to affect change as he was able. He was, after all, a leader.

In his war memoirs written in the mid-1950s de Gaulle referenced the burgeoning menace of Nazi Germany as it related to the book. "As no one proposed anything that would deal with the situation, I felt myself required to appeal to public opinion. I had to expect that one day the searchlights of public life would be directed upon me. It was disagreeable for me to make up my mind to this, after 25 years of living according to military standards."[15]

Of course, military standards had often become an impediment to the greater good as de Gaulle saw it. Such roadblocks had to be removed, and *Vers l'Armée de Métier* was the best the outspoken but obscure lieutenant colonel could offer at the time. Although he had built his own ideas on the foundation of those of others, he must be credited as the foremost, if not the only, officer in the French military who actively sought to change the status quo as it related to battlefield tactics. Others may have agreed, but little more than talk had taken place prior to de Gaulle's effort, and to his credit the soldier with the vast ego never claimed that the concepts were his alone. De Gaulle had been strongly encouraged by Mayer and became a fast friend of the old colonel who had been so influential.

In *Vers l'Armée de Métier,* de Gaulle first discusses the importance of planning and preparing for contingencies due to the continuous ebb and flow of battle. This is followed by a discourse on the character necessary to lead and to command. Then the author describes the mechanization necessary to achieve victory. Four thousand tanks and six divisions of infantry, each man with a six-year contract of service, would be sufficient to present "an awesome system of mechanical skill, gunfire, shock, speed and camouflage.... The troops of today are the machines, coupled with teams trained to serve them.... A liking for what is clean, clipped, compact, this is the driving force behind our highly trained and vigorous youth. But how can it subsist in an army which is perpetually condemned to 'getting by'?"

The opportunity to take a shot at the old-line military men was irresistible, and predictably the book further alienated Charles from some other career officers, particularly powerful members of the general staff and the cadre of the École Supérieure de Guerre, which he still despised. Curiously, although Colonel Mayer was even a greater proponent of air power than of armor, de Gaulle devoted little of the effort to command of the skies. His proposed organizational structure for a first-line armored division, however, was quite detailed.

Each division would consist of several components, including brigades of armor, motorized infantry, and artillery. An armored brigade would include two regiments, one of heavy and the second of medium tanks. A light tank battalion would be attached for reconnaissance. A motorized infantry brigade would consist of two regiments of regular infantry and a battalion of light infantry. An artillery brigade with heavy howitzers of 155mm and a light gun regiment with 75mm cannon would include antiaircraft elements as well. Support troops would consist of an engineer battalion, a logistics battalion, a headquarters group, and other units as needed.

A number of those who bothered to comment on de Gaulle's organization argued that it was counter to France's interests to field an army with such obviously offensive capabilities. Further, the proposed division structure was actually much larger than most believed practical. Although the overriding idea was for speed, its coordinated movement would be a ponderous and quite slow event at best.

General Maurice Gamelin, commander-in-chief of the army, derided the idea of mobile warfare. "I do not believe in Colonel de Gaulle's theories," he said. "They are unsound and unrealistic. Tanks are necessary, it is true. But to think that with tanks you can crush the whole organization of the enemy is just not serious.... The tank is not endowed with self sufficiency. It has to go through, but it has to come back for more fuel and ammunition. As for the air force, it will be a flash in the pan."

Soon enough, much of de Gaulle's theory of modern warfare would be vindicated. Gamelin himself would face humiliating defeat at the hands of the Germans in spring of 1940, and the most prominent weapon in the Nazi arsenal was indeed the tank, supported by fast-moving motorized infantry. For now, however, de Gaulle was relieved of his position with the Supreme Council by the Minister of War, General Louis Maurin, and transferred to the 507th Tank Regiment at Metz with the stinging rebuke, "You have caused us enough trouble with the tank on paper. Now let's see what you can make of the real thing!... Good bye de Gaulle! Wherever I am there will be no room for you." This was followed by an offhand comment to a group of officers gathered around—"I'll send him to Corsica!"[16]

De Gaulle did have at least one ally in government, and in the spring of 1935 Paul Reynaud, one of the few visionary politicians active at the time, presented de Gaulle's proposed mobile army structure to the national assembly. If necessary, de Gaulle had shown that he could be persuasive, and Reynaud recalled of their first meeting on December 5, 1934, that the officer was a "tall lieutenant colonel of light infantry, quietly self confident.... He spoke in an even tone, his voice surprisingly gentle in that great body of his, leaning his face forward. One felt that he was imbued with an irresistibly evident truth."[17]

Although the proposal was defeated soundly in the national assembly, Reynaud spoke of the danger that lay ahead. He remarked,

> Hitler's Germany is raising up a younger generation that has been rendered fanatical and over-excited by all the means of modern publicity, a youth that has been taught that although there is no longer any hope in peace, there may still be hope in war. Can our military organization suffice for the needs of a Europe that has been totally transformed? No, gentlemen. Why not? Because war is a duel in which the attacker alone chooses his weapons.

The French problem, from the military point of view, is the creation of a specialized corps capable of delivering a return blow as shattering as the attack; for if the assaulted does not possess a riposte as rapid as the assailant's, all is lost. Furthermore, our foreign policy absolutely requires us to have this striking force. One must have the army of one's policy. Have we by any chance abandoned the policy of assistance and pacts? Do we wish to change our policy—which we have a right to do—and let Hitler walk about Europe as he chooses?[18]

De Gaulle and Reynaud would remain associated with one another, particularly during the difficult days of May and June 1940. In 1936, when de Gaulle's name reached the promotion list for full colonel, the move was blocked by General Gamelin. Reynaud intervened, but it was not until late 1937 that it was finally approved despite strenuous objections from high-ranking officers. The publication of *Vers l'Armée de Métier* in an official army magazine was also suppressed due to content that the military establishment considered radical.

Despite such hostility to de Gaulle, the officer corps of the French army had begun to grudgingly acknowledge the need for armored divisions. A major military parade was held in Berlin in the spring of 1937, and those who witnessed the vanguard of a fully equipped German panzer division on the move with a covering umbrella of combat aircraft were impressed. Rather than adopting de Gaulle's proposed structure, studies of the tank's capabilities were conducted and more were ordered from arms manufacturers.

The newly constituted armored divisions of the French army would consist of a pair of mixed brigades of three tank battalions, two infantry battalions, an artillery regiment of 36 guns with antiaircraft and antitank support, and reconnaissance, signal, and engineer battalions. Two armored divisions, slightly modified from the original structure, were approved for formation in December 1938, and the first armored brigade was authorized on September 2, 1939, a single day before France declared war on Germany.

Although a great deal of de Gaulle's assertions concerning mobile warfare were proven correct, his ideas are often purported to have played a much greater role in the advent of armored divisions and the refinement of mobile warfare tactics in other armies than actually occurred. Gaullist historians have stated that German General Heinz Guderian, the father of the blitzkrieg, was profoundly influenced by de Gaulle during the prewar years. However, the evidence which supports such a claim is hearsay at best. Others go as far as to say that much of the French officer's theory was his alone. Even de Gaulle stopped short of such a position.

Regardless, the entire affair is further evidence of de Gaulle's indisputable qualities of leadership. Fully aware of the probable response to his work, he was willing to go it alone if necessary, placing his career in a precarious position. Why? He was convinced that he was right. He was determined to stay the course. He refused to acquiesce and simply cooperate for the sake of expediency. Whatever may be said of his irascible personality and soaring ego, the power of perseverance and conviction would serve him well during the difficult days to come.

Lieutenant Colonel de Gaulle reached the 507th Tank Regiment in October 1937. While it was his first real experience with tanks in the field, he understood that the fundamental weakness was in the deployment of the machines, not in the tanks themselves. French tanks were actually among the best in the world and every bit a match for those in the German panzer divisions. However, the French tanks were organized as components of infantry divisions rather than in armored divisions, which France had only just begun to develop.

The 507th Regiment consisted of a battalion of Renault R35 light tanks that mounted a 37mm cannon and a machine gun for defense against enemy infantry along with a battalion of the Renault D2 heavy tank, which mounted a 47mm cannon along with a secondary armament of two machine guns. These tanks were substantial machines, weighing 12 and 20 tons respectively. Characteristically, de Gaulle busied his command with training and drill. Soon enough, the wear and tear on the tanks had begun to show and maintenance costs increased substantially.

During this period, he earned the nickname "Colonel Motor" and drove his command with energy and enthusiasm. Simulated charges and counter-charges were conducted. Within weeks, the 507th Regiment demonstrated with a roaring advance into the center of the city of Metz, 80 tanks in a splendid review of armored fighting power.

As de Gaulle began to implement the principles he had advocated for so long, he wrote to Colonel Mayer, "After a few detailed experiments, I am more than ever convinced of the soundness of the ideas which I have tried to disseminate and which alas have hitherto been accepted much more willingly by the Germans than by my fellow countrymen. Maneuver and attack on land can no longer be required of anything but tanks. What remains is to acknowledge this and then to reorganize the French army accordingly by setting up an instrument for maneuver and assault based on tanks, that is to say an 'armored corps.' "[19]

Through all his tribulation, Charles de Gaulle had never lost the urge to write. Just before his appointment to command the 507th Tank Regiment, he had become acquainted with the author Henri Petiot, whose works, including the 1934 novel *Death, Where Is Thy Victory?*, appeared under the pen name of Henri Daniel-Rops. The two had met as mutual friends of Colonel Mayer. Petiot read some of de Gaulle's previous efforts, and when he came upon the opportunity to commission a book on the military craft he remembered the officer's talent. In short order, de Gaulle had committed himself to producing a volume for a series of books being coordinated for a publishing house by Petiot.

The demands on a regimental commander's time made delivering on the terms of his contract a difficult task for de Gaulle, who suggested an alternative. Over the years, he had kept a copy of the manuscript of *Le Soldat*, which Pétain had declined to see through to publication. A decade had passed since the ghostwriting confrontation, and the two men had actually exchanged cordial letters. Pétain might be willing to allow the publication of a book that included portions of de Gaulle's work on *Le Soldat*.

In April 1938, Charles delivered a manuscript to the publishing house. It was accepted, and a new contract was signed the following month. It is unclear whether Pétain had been informed of anything at this point; however, as far as de Gaulle was concerned the die was cast. At length, de Gaulle was known to have written to the marshal in August of that year requesting approval for the publication of *La France et Son Armée*.

The response from Pétain was swift and unequivocal. "You tell me of the forthcoming publication of a book entitled *La France et Son Armée*. If I understand rightly you intend to use the survey with which I formerly entrusted you in this publication. This I find perfectly astonishing. My surprise can surely not seem unexpected."[20]

The opinion of Pétain had not changed. The writing had been the work of an officer under the direction of the marshal, performed in the offices of his staff. Pétain reasoned that the content belonged to him "since I ordered it to be carried out and directed the writing.... It is my opinion that this work belongs personally and exclusively to me. I, therefore, reserve the right to make use of it as I may think fit. I also reserve the right to oppose its publication now and in the future. In the event of your disregarding this legitimate wish to dispose of the work as I think proper, I make all reservations as to the manner in which I shall act. I find your attitude most distressing."

Two weeks after receiving the marshal's reply, de Gaulle responded that the majority of *La France et Son Armée* had been written after he departed from Pétain's staff and that the remainder had been sufficiently reworded to be construed solely as written by de Gaulle. Following a letter to Pétain that was quite assertive, even by de Gaulle's standards, he softened his attitude a bit.

Pétain had expressed dismay over the fact that publication of the book had reached an advanced stage before he was informed and then suggested that he be allowed to review it and determine what amount of credit he should receive upon publication. De Gaulle agreed that an appropriate acknowledgment of the marshal's involvement should be included in the preface. A meeting was arranged at the marshal's home.

Years later, de Gaulle told conflicting versions of the final time the two men actually sat down with one another in a verbal exchange of any consequence. In the first version, de Gaulle recalled that the meeting had taken place on a Sunday with only the two men present. Pétain was remembered to have said that he had no objection to the publication of the book and asked simply enough that his role in its development be acknowledged. De Gaulle then agreed, and the two parted company.

De Gaulle's second version states that Pétain asked for the proofs in order to review them. When de Gaulle refused, he was ordered to leave them. He responded to Pétain, "You can give me orders in military matters, but not on the literary level."

Whichever is correct, the final blow fell when Pétain sent a draft of a dedication, which de Gaulle chose to ignore. Instead, he had sent the publisher the following: "To Monsieur le Maréchal Pétain, Who wished this book to be written, Whose advice guided the writing of the first five chapters, And thanks to whom the last two are the history of our victory."[21]

When Pétain was informed that de Gaulle had declined to use his version of the dedication, he was enraged and contacted the publishers demanding that his version be substituted. Further, Pétain claimed that some of de Gaulle's facts were in error. De Gaulle was reported to have agreed to substitute the dedication in the second edition of the book, but before a new edition could be published war came in September 1939.

The two men saw one another rarely after their bitter disagreement. When Pétain declined to speak to him during an event at Metz in the autumn of 1938, de Gaulle observed, "The old man is losing his sense of proportion. Nothing and nobody will stop the marshal on the road to senile ambition. Old age is a shipwreck."[22]

By the time of the rupture, the Nazis had been girding for war for six years. De Gaulle, who had seen the coming of another war with Germany, was now more isolated than ever. He had broken with his mentor and was considered a heretic by the senior commanders of the army in which he served. For all his mighty effort, he had been unable to persuade anyone of real consequence that the bleakest of days lay just ahead for France.

Undaunted, de Gaulle managed to look toward an uncertain future, uncertain for his country, his family, and himself. On the eve of World War II, he was in the province of Alsace, commanding the tanks of the Fifth army in support of the fixed fortifications of the Maginot Line.

In command of the French 4th Armored Division, de Gaulle presents his unit to President Albert Lebrun on October 29, 1939. (Photo courtesy of the National Archives and Records Administration)

On Bastille Day, July 14, 1940, de Gaulle inspects French troops in London. (Photo courtesy of the National Archives and Records Administration)

De Gaulle presents medals to Free French soldiers during ceremonies in November 1941. (Photo courtesy of the National Archives and Records Administration)

During the 1942 Casablanca Conference, (left to right) French Army General Henri Giraud, President Franklin D. Roosevelt, General Charles de Gaulle, and Prime Minister Winston Churchill confer. (Photo courtesy of the Library of Congress)

De Gaulle surveys the front line positions of the Allied Fifth Army. (Photo courtesy of the National Archives and Records Administration)

De Gaulle visits with retired US General John J. Pershing, who led the US Army expeditionary force in France during World War I. (Photo courtesy of the National Archives and Records Administration)

De Gaulle is greeted by British General Sir Henry Maitland Wilson, commander of Allied forces in the Mediterranean, upon his arrival at Allied headquarters in Algiers, April 26, 1944. (Photo courtesy of the National Archives and Records Administration)

De Gaulle, followed by US Ambassador to France Jefferson Caffery, arrives at Orly airport in Paris on September 24, 1945. The aircraft is a C-54 transport presented to de Gaulle by US President Harry Truman. (Photo courtesy of the National Archives and Records Administration)

On the day of the liberation of Paris, August 24, 1944, General Charles de Gaulle stands at center on the Champs-Élysées with a group of resistance and Free French leaders. (Photo courtesy of the George Peterson, National Capital Historic Sales, Springfield, Virginia)

De Gaulle visits the French city of Coutances in the autumn of 1945. (Photo courtesy of the National Archives and Records Administration)

De Gaulle arrives for a conference on the rue St. Dominique in Paris, November 22, 1945. (Photo courtesy of the National Archives and Records Administration)

De Gaulle addresses a crowd at Rethondes on March 5, 1948. (Photo courtesy of the National Archives and Records Administration)

De Gaulle answers questions during a Paris press conference on November 12, 1947. (Photo courtesy of the National Archives and Records Administration)

Dressed in military uniform, President Charles de Gaulle shakes hands with US military officers in August 1964 during ceremonies to mark the twentieth anniversary of the invasion of southern France during World War II. (Photo courtesy of the French Tourism Office, New York)

CHAPTER 5

Soul of France

FOR THOSE WHO HAD SEEN THE SIGNS, THE COMING OF WORLD WAR II was no great shock. Since ascending to power in Germany in 1933, Adolf Hitler had defied the Treaty of Versailles, built the German war machine into a colossus, and, like a cancer, spread his territorial claims across the Rhineland, the Sudetenland, Austria, and subsequently all of Czechoslovakia. There was no course remaining for the insatiable Nazi dictator, save waging a war of continuing conquest.

Even before the rise of the Nazis, Charles de Gaulle had warned that another war with Germany was inevitable and that France must exert all energy in preparation for that war. By the autumn of 1938 when the governments of Great Britain and France signed the infamous Munich Pact and the doctrine of appeasement had come to full flower, he was unsurprised but lamented, "France has ceased to be a great nation."

Indeed, the government of Prime Minister Edouard Daladier seemed powerless to act on its own initiative. Without British approval and support, there would be no decisive action taken by the French on the continent of Europe. The small nations of Europe had reason to cower before the Nazi jackboot. France had confirmed that it had no resolve to come to their defense.

Charles wrote to his mother,

> Without a fight we are surrendering to the insolent demands of the Germans and we are handing our allies the Czechs over to the common enemy. German and Italian money has been flooding into the French papers these last days, particularly those that are called "nationalist"...to persuade our poor people that we have to give up. The French, like fools, utter cries of joy, while the German troops march triumphantly into the territory of a state that we built up ourselves. Little by little we are growing accustomed to withdrawal and humiliation, so much that it is becoming second nature to us. We shall drink the cup to its dregs.[1]

When the German juggernaut rolled across the Polish frontier on September 1, 1939, de Gaulle observed with a blend of dread and awe as the mechanized units of the Nazis swept forward and subdued the Poles within weeks. The signing of a non-aggression pact by the Nazis and Soviet Russia, which was followed months later by the Red Army invasion of Poland from the east, was not a shocking turn of events.

"Poland was smashed in a fortnight by the panzer divisions and the Luftwaffe," he wrote in his memoirs. "No doubt the Polish rout was speeded up by Soviet intervention. But Stalin's decision to gang up with Hitler had clearly been dictated by his conviction that the French would not budge, that the Reich had a free hand in the East, and that it was preferable for Russia to share in the spoils than to become Hitler's victim herself."[2]

Although the French government had progressed to the point of at least authorizing the formation of armored divisions in December 1938, the pace of their formation was appallingly slow. Further study was recommended, and the delays were seemingly endless. While de Gaulle watched the rapid advance of German tanks through Poland, he was once again compelled to raise an alarm, writing an analysis of the difficulties the French army would experience in attempting to defend the nation's territory against multiple mobile and armored thrusts.

The recipient of the report was General Dufieux, the same officer who had commanded the École Supérieure during the controversy over de Gaulle's less than stellar graduation rating. Now the inspector general of infantry and tanks, Dufieux discounted the report's findings and appraised, "These conclusions, in the present state of the question, are to be rejected."

As it was, de Gaulle had been appointed to command of the tanks of the Fifth Army just the day before France and Great Britain declared war on Germany in response to the invasion of Poland. Although he had received a substantial promotion, the tanks he was commanding had yet to be organized into formations of rapid movement. The five battalions were not intended to form a cohesive unit; therefore, their firepower, maneuverability, and shock value were minimized. When war came, the armored divisions existed largely on paper. Not until early 1940 would the execution of the order of December 1938 be set in motion.

At least one battalion of de Gaulle's tanks, the 24th, had been involved in a raid against a German position near Schweix, but little military action of consequence occurred along the entire Western Front as autumn slipped into winter. The so-called Phony War offered some the false hope that the shooting might be miraculously minimal, that cooler heads might prevail. Soldiers of both sides eyed one another, blared propaganda through loudspeakers, drilled and engaged in exercises, but rarely fired a weapon. In truth, this was the calm before the storm.

De Gaulle realized that the flawed doctrine of the French military had doomed his country to defeat. Although the Char B1 bis heavy tank was a powerful weapon and more than a match for anything the Germans could send against it, the outcome was a foregone conclusion since it could not be deployed in suitable numbers and coordinated effectively with infantry and artillery. Communications were generally poor between the machines as well. Few had radios, and hand signals and couriers were required to affect the most basic of maneuvers.

Reynaud, one of de Gaulle's few political allies, had been endorsed as prime minister by a single vote on March 21 following the collapse of the Daladier government. He called de Gaulle to Paris to assist in crafting a speech he was to deliver to the national assembly. The address de Gaulle prepared was brief and to the point, calling upon the members of the assembly to rally in support of the all-out war in which France was engaged.

Reynaud prodded that the stake in a total war is exactly that—total. He further asserted the French government and people were duty bound to redouble their efforts and direct all the resources of France to fight the Germans.

De Gaulle believed that changes within the government at the eleventh hour might bring some positive redirection of the course of events during the war. Reynaud, however, was in a precarious political position and forced to cobble together a coalition. Therefore, he retained Daladier in the government as minister of defense and appointed other political adversaries to key positions. No doubt, de Gaulle was dismayed by what he considered a lost opportunity. Further, when Reynaud sought to name him as secretary of France's war committee, Daladier blocked the appointment.

Soon after the outbreak of hostilities, General Gamelin had located his headquarters at the Chateau de Vincennes a short distance from Paris. He rarely ventured away from the luxury of the locale and remained well behind the front lines. Communications with his subordinate commanders were almost nonexistent. Dispatch riders on motorcycles were the most efficient means of communication available.

De Gaulle later received a somewhat curious invitation to lunch at the chateau. Gamelin was certainly aware of the success of German armored divisions in Poland, and recent events undoubtedly prompted him to authorize two additional armored divisions for the French army, bringing the total number to four. De Gaulle was, in fact, to be given command of one of these formations in mid-May. Even so, the hour was late, the days of a polite war in the West were numbered, and de Gaulle knew it.

"Whatever my general feelings about our perhaps irremediable lateness in respect to mechanized forces," he wrote in his memoirs, "I felt very proud at finding myself called upon, as a colonel, to command a division. I said so to General Gamelin. He replied simply: 'I understand your satisfaction. As for your misgivings, I don't believe they are justified.'"[3]

By this time, de Gaulle had already taken an unprecedented step, bold but not in the least out of character for a man of deep conviction. On January 24, 1940, he sent a criticism and analysis of the war in Poland to a collection of 80 senior military officers and civilian politicians.

"In the present conflict to be passive is to admit defeat," he wrote to them. "The French people must at no cost labor under the illusion that the present military immobility would be consistent with the nature of the present war. The opposite is true. The internal combustion engine has given to modern methods of destruction a power, a speed and a range of action such that the present conflict will sooner or later be marked by movement, surprise, invasion, and pursuit, the volume and speed of which will infinitely exceed that of the most astounding events of the past."

De Gaulle entertained a number of visitors at the headquarters of the Fifth Army. Among these was a gathering of members of the

British Parliament. He welcomed the dignitaries and said to them, "Gentlemen, this war is lost.... We must therefore prepare ourselves for another one which will be won with the machine."[4]

He had also maintained an ongoing correspondence with Reynaud. On May 3, a week before the German attack on France and the Low Countries, he exhorted the prime minister to steel the government and the people of France for the debacle that loomed in the near future and to effect needed changes in French military thinking once and for all.

"The events in Norway, following those in Poland, demonstrate that today no military enterprise is possible except in the function and on the scale of available mechanized forces," he advised.

> The French military system is conceived, organized, armed and commanded on the opposite principle of this law of modern warfare. There is no necessity more absolute or more urgent than that of radically reforming this system. The military because of its inherent conformity will not reform itself on its own.
>
> This is above all an affair of state. A statesman is needed.... You alone...by reason of your situation, your personality, and the position you have taken in this matter, and taken alone during the past six years, can and must see the task through. I will take the liberty of adding that in making this question the major concern of your government and in the country would bring into play trump cards that have not yet been used. From now on, each day that passes, each event, helps our doctrine, but, alas, also aids the enemy, who is also putting it into practice.
>
> I hardly need to say that I have no greater ambition than the honor of serving you in this capital undertaking as soon as you judge that the moment has arrived for it.[5]

When the storm finally broke on May 10, 1940, German spearheads knifed into the Netherlands, Belgium, Luxembourg, and France. French war planners, with Pétain chief among them, had strongly asserted that the Ardennes Forest, a heavily wooded area of northeastern France with few good roads and steep terrain, would be an impossible route of attack for the enemy. However, the Germans had planned differently.

The initial German offensive operations moved into the Low Countries, prompting Gamelin to authorize the advance of French divisions and the British Expeditionary Force into Belgium to confront the attackers. The Germans then unleashed 16 divisions, 10 armored, and 6 of mechanized infantry, through the Ardennes. Two French armies, the Second and Ninth, were virtually destroyed. In less than a week, the Germans had outflanked the Maginot Line, crossed the river Meuse, and captured Sedan. German tanks and troops were dashing for the French coastline and the English Channel, trapping thousands of British and French soldiers to the north and eventually pushing them into a small defensive perimeter around the port city of Dunkirk.

Gamelin's plan for the defense of France had unraveled in a matter of days, and he was replaced by General Maxime Weygand. Meanwhile, on May 11, Colonel de Gaulle dutifully arrived at Le Vésinet to take command of the 4th Armored Division. The division itself was still assembling, being put together from units scattered across France.

Hours after the German offensive had begun, de Gaulle wrote a brief letter to his wife. "So the war, the real war, has begun. Yet I should be quite surprised if the present operations in the Netherlands and Belgium really prove to be the great Franco-German battle. In my opinion that will come somewhat later. In any case I should like the 4th Armored Division to be ready as early as possible."[6]

Once again, he was proven correct. When the Germans had achieved their breakthrough, the French generals assumed that their objective was Paris. De Gaulle and the nearly nonexistent 4th Armored Division were ordered to attack the flank of the advancing Germans, buying time for the Sixth Army to vacate its positions on the Maginot Line and establish defenses along the river Aisne to block a German advance on the French capital.

By May 16, de Gaulle had reached the village of Bruyeres, near Laon, with three armored brigades, less than half his prescribed strength in tanks. Along the way, he was dismayed to see long lines of French soldiers without weapons and streaming toward the rear. These were soldiers of a beaten army. It was there, amid the chaos of the moment, that de Gaulle made a momentous personal decision. He would not surrender, whatever the circumstances. He would fight to the end.

"Miserable processions of refugees crowded along all the roads from the north," he wrote in his memoirs.

> I also saw a number of troops who had lost their weapons. They belonged to the troops routed by the panzers during the preceding day. Caught up as they fled by the enemy's mechanized detachments, they had been ordered to throw away their arms and make off to the south so as not to clutter up the roads.
>
> "We haven't time," they had been told, "to take you prisoner!"
>
> Then, at the sight of those bewildered people and of those soldiers in rout, at the tale, too, of that contemptuous piece of insolence of the enemy's, I felt myself borne up by a limitless fury. "Ah, it is too stupid. The war is beginning as badly as it could. Therefore, it must go on. For this, the world is wide. If I live, I will fight, wherever I must, as long as I must, until the enemy is defeated and the national stain washed clean." All I have managed to do since has resolved upon that day.

To say that the 4th Armored Division was inexperienced would be an understatement. Some of the troops had never participated in maneuvers. Officers took command of their units and were marching toward the Germans within hours. Nevertheless, de Gaulle set about assessing the situation and determining how to carry out his orders. Reconnaissance reports convinced the commanding officer that the Germans were not driving on Paris but instead toward St. Quentin, a crossing of the river Somme, and the English Channel.

Spurred to action, he decided that the village of Montcornet, several miles distant, would serve as a reasonable objective. Holding the crossroads town would delay the Germans for some time. He ordered his tanks to fan out along both sides of the road from Laon and moved forward around 4:30 on the morning of May 17. By noon, the first of nearly 100 French tanks had reached Montcornet and engaged elements of the German 1st Panzer Division.

The Germans were taken by surprise, and in the confusion some advanced infantry squads were cut off and captured. By the end of the day, about 120 Germans had been taken prisoner. As de Gaulle's command moved forward, an infantry battalion that had been under his command in Germany in 1927 arrived and went into action against a pocket of enemy troops which had been bypassed by the faster-moving French tanks.

For a time, the Germans had been unable to determine the size and strength of the force that had hit their flank and threatened lines of communication and supply. The unexpected French attack did cause some moments of confusion.

The 4th Armored Division had lost only 25 killed and wounded, but 23 tanks had been destroyed or disabled. There were no additional troops to follow up and hold the ground gained. German artillery was beginning to pound the French forces occupying Montcornet, and Junkers Ju-87 Stuka dive bombers were attacking as well. De Gaulle's orders had been specific—to fight a delaying action—and he had accomplished this as best he could. That evening the French pulled back to their original starting positions.

Some Gaullist historians have assigned greater significance than is warranted to the action at Montcornet, weaving a yarn that the 4th Armored Division actually halted the German spearheads, which were under the command of General Heinz Guderian, a foremost proponent of the blitzkrieg, or Lightning War, which included the coordination of aircraft, armor, and fast-moving infantry. As noted, the Germans were not marching on Paris. They had halted on orders from Hitler, who feared that the rapid advance of the tanks had left them exposed. Nevertheless, de Gaulle's command had performed quite well in the most difficult circumstances.

The following day, two additional regiments reached the 4th Armored Division at Laon and raised the total available tanks to about 150. On May 19, the French struck at the bridges across the river Serre close to the historic town of Crécy and nearby Pouilly, north of Laon. The Germans were expecting action this time, and the Stukas rained bombs on the French tanks and infantry.

De Gaulle watched the progress of this attack from the hill of Mont Fendu, observing its high tide when the advance reached within a mile of a German command post. Guderian later mentioned that he had experienced several hours of uncertainty that day, but in the end the French attack was an exercise in futility. In the late afternoon, de Gaulle had personally driven to the headquarters of the Sixth Army to request additional troops, but this overture was brushed aside. During the following day, he disengaged and began retiring to the south. As Guderian advanced, his panzers crossed the Somme and captured the cities of Abbeville and Amiens on May 20.

De Gaulle was promoted to the temporary rank of brigadier general on May 21, and by the 22nd his command was called upon once more. This time the 4th Armored Division was to relocate some 150 miles to the west to contest the German advance beyond Abbeville. Such a movement would have been difficult during wartime for an experienced unit to accomplish, but its strength also increased during that time with the addition of antiaircraft and artillery formations.

On May 27, de Gaulle had reached Abbeville and determined that an attack against the German bridgehead across the river Somme would be the appropriate course of action. The fighting began in earnest on May 28 and lasted for three days. The French could call upon no reinforcements. The Germans held command of the skies, relieved battle-weary troops with fresh soldiers, and managed to hold their crossing.

The attack against Abbeville is thought to have gained anywhere from five to 14 miles of territory and did in fact shrink the size of the German bridgehead, while somewhere from 250 to 400 German prisoners were taken. After the first day's action, the morale of the French troops was reportedly high, and the tablecloth in de Gaulle's headquarters was said to have been a captured Nazi flag adorned with the hated swastika.

For all their bravery, however the French attempt to capture Abbeville itself and eliminate the lodgment had failed, just as a prior attack by British forces had. Estimates of the available French tank strength at the beginning of the attack range from 140 to 160, about one-third of which were the heavy Char B1 bis with a formidable 75mm main gun. French tank losses were estimated to be as low as 70 and possibly greater than 130, which would have left the entire division with fewer than 30 operational armored vehicles.

Although the Germans were reported to have had ample reinforcements at their disposal, the brunt of the fighting was borne by two battalions of infantry. The superb handling of 88mm flak guns positioned inside the bridgehead and used in the antitank role quite probably sealed the fate of the attack and took a heavy toll in French tanks.

The official history of the 4th Armored Division relates that its commanding officer was during the Abbeville engagement "always in the front line, often among the advance reconnaissance units, with his headquarters exposed to enemy fire; if it was a question of an attack he refused to listen to the slightest objection, even if it was well founded. One saw his leather jacket, his helmet with the eternal cigarette underneath it, everywhere. Day and night did not count. He was not easy to approach or easy to live with. He was haughty and serious, spoke little. If one asked him a question one got a rebuke. As in the First World War he disdained the slightest precaution. Although he had no air support and his tanks were subject to constant attacks by Stukas, he always stood with the hatch of his own tank open and, if on his feet, refused to notice bombs and thundered at anyone who threw themselves on the ground."[7]

After the war, one of de Gaulle's junior officers who was near the division commander throughout the fighting at Abbeville wrote his own account of the battle, providing further insight into de Gaulle as a leader on the battlefield.

"By May 28 we had traveled about 200 kilometers in six days," the officer remembered.

General de Gaulle decided to attack toward Mont-de-Caubert at 5 p.m. The tanks were slow in coming together, and then it seemed to me that they were too close together. The enemy had a great many very well placed anti-tank weapons, and they inflicted heavy losses upon us. But by the evening we had taken Huppy and there we were at Mont-de-Limeux, from which the Germans had fled in disorder leaving their supper in their traveling kitchens. We took 400 prisoners!

At 4 a.m. the general launched the second attack. The sky was overcast, the enemy planes less effective, and our artillery had been reinforced. We made our way into Huchenneville; some of our tanks reached Mont-de-Caubert. We received a signal that enemy columns were hurriedly crossing back over the Somme. Abbeville was within our reach. But the enemy counterattacked in the Villers wood. The villages we had taken, Bienfant for example, were heavily shelled. General de Gaulle went up to the firing line and summoned his colonels. "Colonel de Ham, you are at Bienfant. You will hold the village until tomorrow. Colonel Francois, you are at Mesnil-trois-Foetus. You will hold out until tomorrow morning."

We spent a short night at the chateau of Huppy, where the wounded were being tended and which the enemy shelled. At dawn, a messenger came to tell de Gaulle that Colonel Francois had been killed. The general's only reaction was, "Who will replace him?" And the attack on Mont-de-Caubert began again the same day. But the division could not take Abbeville. It had reached the limit of its powers.[8]

Detached and emotionless, de Gaulle gave no hint of the passion and anguish that raged within him. He did not take a moment to mourn the dead. France herself was in mortal danger. General Alphonse Georges, who commanded all French ground forces engaged that fateful spring, testified in 1946 during a formal inquiry as to the reasons for the collapse of the French military in the face of the German onslaught. "The 4th Armored Division was improvised on the battlefield," he noted. "Yet it was the only one that disorganized the German columns to a considerable extent when it was thrown against their flank. So true is it that the divisions must, out of necessity, be commanded by bold, dynamic leaders who have reflected at length upon the potentialities of these special units in battle. Such was then the case with Colonel de Gaulle."[9]

He may not have been loved by the soldiers he led, but he was certainly respected by them. He did, in fact, lead. In three weeks' time, he had taken command of a combat division that did not even exist as a whole; fought the highly mechanized German army, achieving some small measure of success against it, and salvaging at least a shred of honor for the French military; and been mentioned in the dispatches of the highest-ranking general in the field.

All this had been accomplished primarily due to one man's leadership, drive, and determination. De Gaulle remained undeterred and resolved to fight to the finish. He later wrote, "During those difficult hours, I could not help but imagine what the mechanized army of which I had so long dreamed could have done. If it had been there to debouch suddenly, the advance of the panzer divisions would have been halted instantly, serious confusion caused in the rear areas, and the northern group of our armies enabled to join up once more with those of the center and the east."[10]

Following its relief on May 31 by the British 51st Highland Division, the remnants of de Gaulle's command eventually withdrew to Marseille-en-Beauvaisis. The British and French soldiers trapped to the north made their way to the Channel coast, and more than 350,000 were rescued by a hodgepodge of warships, fishing boats, and pleasure craft that braved Luftwaffe bombing and strafing to bring them safely to Britain. One of the epic events of World War II, the seaborne operation came to be known as the Miracle of Dunkirk.

De Gaulle traveled to Paris on June 1 and visited General Weygand, who informed him that the withdrawal from Dunkirk would include French troops. Weygand further asked de Gaulle for advice on how to effectively deploy several hundred tanks that were still available. De Gaulle replied that they should be grouped into a single corps of three divisions and utilized to attack the overextended German flanks as the panzer spearheads moved south. Immodestly, he proposed himself as commander of this corps. Weygand took no action.

In the meantime, Reynaud had been compelled to appoint Pétain, who had been serving as ambassador to Spain, as deputy prime minister in an attempt to bolster the morale of the people in the face of catastrophic defeat. Along with General Weygand, the marshal was advocating an armistice with the Germans at the earliest possible opportunity. De Gaulle was prompted to write Reynaud, who had been an ardent opponent of the Nazis for some time, urging him to stand up for France and scolding the prime minister for allowing defeatists to occupy positions of responsibility during such a time of peril.

On June 6, the brazen brigadier was awakened to the news that he was to take a position in the Reynaud government. Within 30 minutes the telephone rang at Marseille-en-Beauvaisis, and the prime minister was requesting that he come to Paris as soon as possible and assume the office of undersecretary of state for national defense. A day earlier, the Germans renewed their offensive in France following a week's respite. Charles advised his wife to seek a place to live in Carantec, in the coastal area of Brittany and as far from the fighting as was practical.

Both Pétain and Weygand objected strenuously to the appointment of de Gaulle to even a minor post in the government. Weygand protested, "He is an infant!" Apparently, the age of 50 was not advanced enough in the general's opinion.[11]

Pétain was even more critical, saying, "He thinks he knows all about the mechanics of warfare. His vanity leads him to think the art of war has no secrets for him. He might have invented it. I know all about him. He was once on my staff and wrote a book, or at least I told him to do so. I gave him the outline and corrected it.... When he published it he did not even acknowledge my contribution. Not only is he vain, he is ungrateful. He has few friends in the army. No wonder, for he gives the impression of looking down on everybody."[12]

Although he had pursued a career in the military, Charles de Gaulle was preparing to enter the political arena. The day after his appointment, he visited Reynaud at the war ministry. True enough, the embattled prime minister had attempted to quell the defeatist rhetoric within the government. Daladier had been shuffled to the foreign office, and although Pétain was still prominent Reynaud had reasoned that the old hero was a lesser threat while he remained within the government rather than outside it.

Briefly de Gaulle had considered suggesting that available French forces should be massed in Brittany, constitute a defensive redoubt, and continue fighting the Germans from their homeland. However, he quickly dismissed this far-fetched scheme. Considering the alternatives left to France, he suggested that the government relocate to North Africa and continue the war from there. Reynaud had also been evaluating this contingency plan. Estimates of troop strength that could be transferred there were as high as half a million. The potent French fleet could still exert influence on the outcome of the fight against the Germans, and thousands of colonial troops could be mobilized as well. The cooperation of the British, particularly of the Royal Navy, would be essential in a relocation to North Africa, should this become necessary.

It was agreed that de Gaulle would travel to London, meet Prime Minister Winston Churchill, and assure the British government that France would continue the war from North Africa if necessary, honoring a pledge that the two countries had made not to seek a separate peace with Germany. In the meantime, he would ask for more British aircraft to be moved to France.

As he prepared for his first mission to London, de Gaulle visited Weygand at his headquarters at the Chateau de Montry. The discussion was sobering even for de Gaulle. Weygand pronounced that France was beaten, the Germans would cross the Marne and the Seine Rivers, and that the end was near. He then intoned that Britain would seek peace terms with the Nazis within a week of France's military defeat. Reynaud agreed with de Gaulle that Weygand should be relieved of command but did not act for fear that his shaky government would collapse with discord.

On June 9, Undersecretary de Gaulle flew from Paris to London accompanied by Roland de Margerie, a career diplomat who served as Reynaud's private secretary, and Geoffrey de Courcel, an aide who had just returned from Syria and was newly appointed to de Gaulle. When the French diplomats arrived, Churchill was having a difficult day. He had been informed earlier that fascist Italy was preparing to enter the war and was snapping at staff personnel.

"Mr. Churchill received me in Downing Street," de Gaulle remembered years later. "It was my first contact with him. The impression he gave me confirmed my conviction that Great Britain, led by such a fighter, certainly would not flinch. Mr. Churchill seemed to me to be equal to the rudest task, provided it also had grandeur. The assurance of his judgment, his great culture, the knowledge he had of most of the subjects, countries and men involved, and finally his passion for the problems proper to war, found in war their full scope. On top of everything he was fitted by his character to act, take risks, play the part out and out without scruple. In short, I found him well in the saddle as guide and chief. Such were my first impressions."[13]

De Gaulle's appeal for more fighter planes was sympathetically but firmly turned down. However, one positive by-product of this first meeting with Churchill was the impression the tall brigadier left on the chief of the British government. Churchill found de Gaulle to be a man of staunch resolution, willing to partner with the British in the fight against Nazi Germany, and partner until that fight was finished. He was not cut from the same cloth as those downcast and defeatist French diplomats Churchill had come to know.

The day of his return, June 10, de Gaulle remembered as one of agony. During a meeting with Reynaud and Weygand, the prime minister asked how long it might be until the Germans were in Paris. Their renewed offensive along the River Somme was proceeding rapidly, and French resistance was crumbling. Weygand estimated their arrival in about 24 hours. It was evident that the senior commander favored an armistice.

Reynaud would not give in, and de Gaulle added that there were other options. Weygand, still vehemently opposed to de Gaulle's participation in the government, responded sarcastically, "Have you something to suggest?" De Gaulle coldly answered, "The government does not have suggestions to make, but orders to give. I am sure that it will give them."[14]

Reynaud believed that a capable defense of Paris was a pipe dream, although de Gaulle disagreed. Nevertheless, the prime minister declared the French capital an open city, and the government undertook a rapid evacuation to the south. Documents were destroyed and bags hastily packed. Late in the night on June 10, Reynaud and de Gaulle left Paris for the temporary safety of Orléans to the south and then on to Briare. To compound the difficulty of the day, word was received that at midnight Italy would enter the war on the side of Germany. Belgium had surrendered a few days earlier.

Meanwhile, Weygand (according to de Gaulle years later) overstepped his authority and contacted London to request that Churchill

come to France for a meeting at Briare to discuss the rapidly dete-
riorating situation. De Gaulle demanded that Weygand be relieved
of command and replaced with General Charles Huntziger, who was
willing to take the job. Reynaud, however, fearful of a backlash from
other politicians and military leaders who advocated an armistice,
could not bring himself to relieve the troublesome Weygand.

As the French prepared to receive the British delegation, de
Gaulle and Pétain met for the first time in two years, their last brush
having been when the marshal refused to speak during his visit to
Metz in 1938. "So, you are a general now," Pétain remarked with
some veiled disgust. "I do not congratulate you. What good is rank
in defeat?"[15]

When de Gaulle reminded Pétain that it was during the retreat
of 1914 during World War I that Pétain was first promoted to general
rank, the old marshal muttered something to the effect that the situ-
ations were not comparable. De Gaulle later admitted that at least on
that point the old man had been right.

The meeting with Churchill at Briare on the evening of June 11
produced no tangible results, and de Gaulle had sat through the discussion of the litany of French setbacks without comment. Other talk
centered on the fate of the powerful French fleet and the possible continuation of the fight from somewhere in Brittany, such as de Gaulle
had previously envisaged but discounted. Although he said little or
nothing, de Gaulle's stock did rise with the British delegation.

Major General Sir Edward Spears wrote later, "He was calm, self-
contained, absolutely unflustered. The British civilians and soldiers
were delighted to see that Reynaud had the support of this vigorous
character. The Frenchmen's faces were pale, their eyes fixed on the
table. They really looked like prisoners who had been brought out
of their cells to hear the inevitable verdict. Looking around for a less
discouraging sight, I turned towards de Gaulle. He was the only one
of his compatriots to show a coolness that might be compared to that
of the British."[16]

Interestingly, de Gaulle had been seated close to Churchill during the dinner that followed and carried on a general conversation with the British prime minister concerning recent events. The following day, a second round of discussions took place and left the British with little assurance that the French would continue to fight for very long. The conversation between Churchill and de Gaulle, though, must have made quite an impression on the British leader.

When he had returned to London, the prime minister cabled US president Franklin D. Roosevelt with his impression of the meeting at Briare. "The aged Marshal Pétain is, I fear, ready to lend his name and prestige to a treaty of peace for France. Reynaud, on the other hand, is for fighting on, and he has a young General de Gaulle who believes much can be done."[17]

As de Gaulle made contingency plans for the French government to relocate to North Africa, possibly Algiers, Reynaud bowed to pressure from his ministers and agreed to move the government to Bordeaux rather than the location de Gaulle had favored, the town of Quimper. Those in favor of armistice had insisted on Bordeaux, and Reynaud issued a communiqué to Weygand to continue the struggle against the Germans while the government would evacuate by sea if this last-ditch effort failed. Reynaud did not identify any specific destination should the evacuation become necessary, while de Gaulle had reasoned that the government would have moved to North Africa more easily from Quimper.

Cries for an armistice with Germany were growing louder. Of course, there was the matter of French honor. The agreement with Great Britain that neither country would pursue a separate peace, however, seemed irrelevant to some at this dire moment. Reynaud requested another meeting with Churchill, and this time the two met on the afternoon of June 13 at Tours. Although Reynaud may have appeared more resolute just two days earlier, the purpose of this meeting appears to have been to sound the British response to an appeal for terms from the Germans.

Understandably, Reynaud did not want de Gaulle present and did not inform the undersecretary of the meeting. When a member of Reynaud's staff informed de Gaulle that Churchill was at Tours, Charles sped to the town and reached the prefecture where the meeting was taking place just as it was recessing. While de Gaulle was absent, Reynaud had informed the British that Weygand was convinced that overtures for an armistice should be made to the Germans. How, then, would the British react?

Churchill replied in somewhat broken French, "I understand that you are going to ask for an armistice. We shall not waste our time in recriminations. The French cause will always be dear to us, and if we win the war we shall reestablish France in all her power and glory. But Great Britain cannot be asked to give up the solemn undertaking that binds the two countries."[18]

De Gaulle had missed this portion of the meeting but arrived in time to hear French reassurances that their powerful fleet would not be allowed to fall into German hands and that German airmen who had been captured by the French would be turned over to the British so that they could not fly against the island nation in the days ahead.

Shocked by what he heard, Charles confronted Reynaud after the proceedings and asked whether he had informed the British that France would seek peace with the Germans. When the prime minister insisted that he had not, the undersecretary had to doubt the truth in his words.

The British had heard enough and began to depart in rather hasty fashion; however, Churchill noticed that de Gaulle was in the room, walked over, shook his hand, and said quietly, "*L'homme du destin* (the man of destiny)."[19] Perhaps these words resonated with de Gaulle and stirred him to further action. No doubt, coming from Churchill the comment was a supreme validation of de Gaulle's character and bearing— and willingness to lead.

De Gaulle once again found himself at a crossroads, or on the edge of the proverbial sword about which he had written years earlier.

It seemed that his foray into politics, although during extraordinary times, had been a dismal failure. Reynaud had not firmly agreed to relocate the government to Algiers or anywhere else in North Africa. Due to concern over the repercussions, he had also failed to relieve Weygand of command. Finally, and most compelling of all, he seemed to be wavering on continuing the war. De Gaulle could not, in good conscience, remain a member of the government that was preparing to sacrifice the honor of France in exchange for a humiliating peace with a haughty enemy. He made up his mind to resign.

As he was writing his letter to Reynaud, de Gaulle was interrupted by Georges Mandel, the Minister of the Interior. Mandel, who had been warned by a member of de Gaulle's staff that he intended to resign, was a Jew and had strongly opposed an armistice. He was later arrested by the Vichy government, turned over to the Germans, who imprisoned him in a concentration camp, sent back to the Vichy authorities two years later, and murdered by their secret police in 1944.

On this night, Mandel was considering the fate of France and concluded that he must persuade de Gaulle to remain in the government, perhaps seeing more clearly even than de Gaulle himself, that this man of destiny would play a pivotal role in the days to come. "In any case we are only at the beginning of the world war," de Gaulle recalled Mandel saying with gravity and resolution. "You will have great duties to perform, general. But you will perform them with the advantage of being the one man among us all, a man with an unblemished reputation. It may emerge that your present position will make things easier for you."[20]

Early on the morning of June 14, 1940, German troops marched triumphantly into Paris, the City of Light, and the prize that had eluded them twice during World War I. Not a shot was fired in the city's defense. Also on that day, de Gaulle once again pressed Reynaud for a decision on moving the government to Algiers. At long last, Reynaud agreed that it was the proper thing to do. He ordered de Gaulle to London to ask the British for full cooperation in the effort.

That evening, de Gaulle waited for an airplane, which never arrived, to take him to London. While he waited, he went to dinner at the Hotel Splendide. At a nearby table sat none other than Pétain. De Gaulle strode over to the marshal's table. The two shook hands but did not exchange a word. It was the last time they were to see one another.

When no plane showed up, de Gaulle and Courcel, his aide, decided to drive through the night and reached Rennes, west of Paris, for a discussion on the defense of Brittany where as many troops as possible could be concentrated at the ports for debarkation to North Africa. From there, Charles stopped briefly to visit his mother, who was dying, at Paimpont. Another short stop was made at Carantec to visit his wife and daughters.

He told Yvonne, "Things are very bad. I am on my way to London. Perhaps we are going to carry on the fight in Africa, but I think more likely that everything is about to collapse. I am warning you so that you will be ready to leave at the first sign."[21]

Finally, on the afternoon of June 15, de Gaulle reached the port of Brest and boarded the French destroyer *Milan,* bound for Plymouth. Once in Great Britain, he was flown to London. When he reached the British capital, he radioed the French cargo ship *Pasteur,* en route to France and laden with war materiel, to dock in a British port to prevent the supplies from falling into German hands. This gesture was well beyond the scope of his authority, and when it was heard of in Bordeaux several ministers called on Reynaud to dismiss de Gaulle or to prefer charges against him.

En route to London, de Gaulle no doubt pondered the future of France and his role in the difficult days ahead. He was reported to have even asked the captain of the French destroyer *Milan* if he would be willing to fight under the British flag. His decision on the *Pasteur* also indicated a growing independence of thought and action.

On the morning of June 16, de Gaulle was shaving in his room at the Hotel Hyde Park in London. He was interrupted by Jean Monnet, who was serving as chairman of the joint Franco-British committee on the economic coordination of the war effort, and Charles Corbin, the French ambassador to Great Britain. They explained that they had been working with British officials to put forward a proposal for an Anglo-French Union. Such a union would assist Reynaud in his efforts to block the defeatists. Although it sounded far-fetched, and it was readily apparent that no document could immediately bind France and Great Britain together as a single nation, de Gaulle took the idea to Churchill.

During lunch with Corbin and the British prime minister at the fashionable Carlton Club, de Gaulle raised the idea of the union. Churchill was already aware of the plan, having been briefed by his own advisers who had been involved in its formation. He advised that previously approved communication with the French acquiesced to their possibly seeking an armistice as long as French warships sailed to British ports and should not be delivered to the Germans, and he called a cabinet meeting for the afternoon of June 16.

Churchill's cabinet deliberated and debated for more than two hours before the prime minister emerged from the meeting and walked into the next room to tell de Gaulle that he should phone Reynaud to offer the union. When he received the news, Reynaud was almost speechless. In turn, he called a meeting of his ministers to discuss the opportunity. As it turned out, the 24 French ministers who assembled did not even vote on the proposal, considering it impossible to conclude. While arrangements were being made to fly de Gaulle back to Bordeaux and for representatives of the two governments to meet about the details, Marshal Pétain muttered that it would be a marriage to a corpse. The cries for an armistice grew louder.

Churchill himself had boarded a train at London's Waterloo Station in company with Monnet and had planned to sail from

Portsmouth to meet with the French delegation that he expected. Before the train pulled away from the station, a messenger arrived with the news that Reynaud would resign and that Pétain had been asked by President Albert Lebrun to form a new government. Churchill wrote later that he returned to 10 Downing Street with a heavy heart.

At 6:30 p.m., de Gaulle boarded a Royal Air Force plane for his return to France. He and Monnet had one more brief discussion with Churchill before his departure, and Monnet renewed the plea for more British fighter planes to be sent to France. Churchill flatly refused. Then, somewhat remarkably, de Gaulle took a couple of steps back and said, "I think you are quite right."

Churchill noted further while observing de Gaulle in that moment, "Under an impassive, imperturbable demeanor he seemed to me to have a remarkable capacity for feeling pain. I preserved the impression, in contact with this very tall, phlegmatic man: 'Here is the Constable of France.'"

With the news that Pétain had been summoned as the new prime minister, de Gaulle was well aware that an order for his own arrest was imminent. He would have to leave France or face imprisonment and possibly a death sentence.[22]

As pressing as making arrangements for his own departure from France were, Charles asked for passports to assure that his wife and children could join him in Britain. Communications had become problematic, and although Yvonne did not actually know where her husband was, she knew of his intent to go across the English Channel in the event of a French collapse. Yvonne and her daughters went to Brest to find an aunt and borrow money to make the passage. Finally, she was able to secure enough francs and 100 pounds sterling. Two ships were in the harbor and taking on passengers for Britain. Luckily, the family missed the first of these to depart. It was sunk. They boarded the last ship and safely reached Plymouth.

When de Gaulle landed in Bordeaux, he went quickly to Reynaud's office and told the former prime minister of his intent to return to London. Reynaud gave de Gaulle 100,000 francs from the government's reserve. It was essentially all the money that was left, and it amounted to about $500. Around midnight, de Gaulle met with General Sir Edward Spears, British military liaison officer to the French government, and British ambassador to France Ronald Campbell in their quarters at the Hotel Montré and told them of his intent to leave France.

De Gaulle had little time to spare. The Germans would arrive in Bordeaux in a matter of days. Since he had no post in the government any longer, he was now an officer in the French army and subject to the vengeance of Weygand, who might place him under arrest—and the Vichy authorities under Pétain were probably already searching for him.

Spears telephoned Churchill and asked for permission to accompany de Gaulle on his flight to London. The request was reluctantly approved because Spears had represented the last official link between the British army and the crumbling French government. The decision was made to drive to the Mérignac airport the following morning. De Gaulle and Courcel, his aide, would make the trip to the airport ostensibly to bid farewell to Spears. At the last moment, they would hop aboard the plane bound for Britain.

The plan for the morning of June 17 was for de Gaulle, Courcel, and Spears to meet in the lobby of the Hotel Normandy about 7:30 and drive to the airport together. Two cars were needed. The second carried the baggage, five pieces in all, which had to be tied to the frame of the biplane, which was painted with RAF roundels and had room for four people, including the pilot, who had slept in his aircraft.

In the confusion of the airport, the small plane was hardly noticed, and the air of excitement surrounding the clandestine departure may have been overblown by history. In fact, Courcel remembered that de Gaulle seemed detached and more concerned with what awaited him on the other side of the Channel than any perceived hazard in the departure. As the men appeared to say goodbye to one another, Spears climbed aboard, and the plane's engine coughed to life. Just as the pilot started to taxi, de Gaulle and Courcel boarded.

De Gaulle remembered, "We flew over La Rochelle and Rochefort. Ships set on fire by German aircraft were burning in these ports. We passed over Paimpont, where my mother lay very ill. The forest was all smoking from the munition dumps which were being destroyed there. After a stop at Jersey, we reached London in the early afternoon. While I was taking rooms and Courcel was telephoning the embassy and the missions and finding them already reticent, I seemed to myself, alone as I was and deprived of everything, like a man on the shore of an ocean proposing to swim across it."[23]

Churchill summed up the one thing de Gaulle did possess. "De Gaulle," he wrote, "carried with him, in this small airplane, the honor of France."[24]

CHAPTER 6

Out of Ashes

IN LEAVING FOR LONDON, DE GAULLE HAD CROSSED HIS PERSONAL Rubicon. With the 84-year-old Pétain in power, he had effectively turned his back on the government of France. By refusing to be a party to an armistice with the Nazis, he had stepped back from much of what he held sacred, including the discharge of his duties as an officer in the French army. He chose exile and had no legitimate claim to authority or to represent his country. He had come to Britain totally dependent on the goodwill of his hosts and until a few days earlier had been an obscure brigadier general.

Considering his situation, de Gaulle later reflected on his intentions while writing his memoirs.

> I was nothing to begin with. But this very destitution pointed out my line of conduct. It was by taking up the cause of national salvation, without troubling about anything else at all, that I might

acquire authority. It was by acting as the unbending champion of the nation and the state that it might be possible for me to gather agreement and even enthusiastic support among the French and to obtain respect and esteem from foreigners. In short, although I was so restricted and alone, and indeed because I was so restricted and alone, I had to reach the heights and never come down again.[1]

After sizing up the situation, de Gaulle was informed that Churchill would meet with him that afternoon. Working under the shade of the trees in the garden at 10 Downing Street, the prime minister greeted the French refugee warmly, and the two men conferred briefly. Each of them wanted to keep France fighting as long as possible, and it was apparent to Churchill that having a Frenchman in London to help cultivate a resistance movement against the Nazis would be a benefit.

The most effective means of reaching and rallying the French people would be by radio broadcast over the BBC, asserted de Gaulle. Churchill agreed, but he had to persuade several members of his war cabinet, who believed that there was no solid ground on which de Gaulle could stand. Britain still maintained relations with the Pétain government, they reasoned, and the more proper course of action might be to see how its negotiations with the Nazis proceeded before allowing de Gaulle access to the BBC.

Churchill disagreed but intended to allow Pétain to add legitimacy to de Gaulle's intended broadcast by announcing his intent to parlay with the Germans. If Pétain made such an announcement, it would be seen as a breach of the agreement with Great Britain and would further rally those Frenchmen who did not share the old marshal's defeatist sentiment. Pétain obliged, broadcasting from Bordeaux on the afternoon of June 17. He intoned, "I give to France my person to assuage her misfortune. It is with a broken heart that I tell you today it is necessary to stop the fighting."[2]

One of de Gaulle's associates in France had given him the keys to a small apartment in London, and there he began to write the text of his address, which would come the following evening. Courcel had already contacted a longtime friend, Elisabeth de Miribel, who was working at the time in the Economics Mission at the French Embassy, and asked her to come to the apartment to do some typing of a very important nature.

De Gaulle wrote and rewrote the text of his address, which came to be known as the Appeal of June 18. Just before 6 p.m., he and Courcel arrived at Broadcasting House, the BBC headquarters. The Frenchmen were greeted by Stephen Tallents, the head of the BBC News.

Elizabeth Barker of the BBC remembered that de Gaulle was "a huge man with highly polished boots, who walked with long strides, talking in a very deep voice...above all, icily contained within himself—not at all what one imagines a Frenchman to be. There was something different about him, different from other men. One could sense that straight away. I don't mean the 'man of destiny' business, but he was most remarkably self-possessed."[3]

When he reached Studio 4B, on the fourth floor of the building, two announcers, Maurice Thierry and Gibson Parker, were present, and Thierry was reading the news. De Gaulle was asked to give a voice level and said only two words, "La France." The level was acceptable.

In that clear, resonating voice for which he was known, de Gaulle delivered his first address to the French nation. Its duration was only about four minutes, and it was given during a time slot generally reserved for a news broadcast to France. The BBC personnel had been given scarcely an hour's notice that de Gaulle was coming, and no arrangements for a recording were made. Few people were reported to have actually heard the appeal as it was broadcast; however, it was reproduced in print.

De Gaulle stared at the microphone and began:

The leaders who have been at the head of the French armies for many years have formed a government.

This government, on the pretext that our armies have been defeated, have made contact with the enemy in order to cease the fight.

Certainly we have been, we are, overwhelmed by the enemy's mechanical strength on land and in the air.

Far more than the numbers of Germans, it is their tanks, their planes, and their tactics which have taken our leaders by surprise and brought them to where they are today.

But has the last word been said? Must hope be abandoned? Is our defeat complete? No!

Believe me when I tell you that nothing is lost for France. I speak in knowledge of the facts. The same means which have defeated us can bring us victory one day.

For France is not alone! She is not alone! She is not alone! She has a great empire behind her. She can unite with the British Empire which rules the seas and is continuing the fight. Like Britain, she can make unlimited use of the immense industrial resources of the United States.

This war is not restricted to the territory of our unhappy country. This war has not been decided by the Battle of France. This war is a world war. All our errors, all our delays, all our sufferings do not alter the fact that the world contains all the resources needed to overwhelm our enemies one day. Struck down today by mechanized might, we can conquer one day in the future by superior mechanized might. The fate of the world turns on that.

I, General de Gaulle, now in London, call on all French officers and soldiers now present on British territory or who may be so in the future, with or without their arms; I call on engineers and specialist workers in the arms industry now present on British territory or who may be so in the future, to get in touch with me.

Whatever happens, the flame of French resistance must not and will not be extinguished.

Tomorrow, as today, I shall speak on the radio from London.

This four-minute appeal, heard by few, and delivered without fanfare, was by no means the commencement of a Free French movement. There was the ring of defiant nationalism, however, and in it the last vestige of any willingness to serve a collaborationist government. The Vichy leaders, preparing to sign an armistice with the Nazis, had ordered their armed forces to cease resistance. An obstinate junior officer had refused these orders, fled to the protection of another country, and was urging others to do the same. Each, in the eyes of the other, had committed high treason.

For the British, June 18 did not present a moment of realization that Charles de Gaulle was the last or even the best hope for rallying the French nation to continue the fight. Actually, Monnet had persuaded Churchill to organize yet another mission to France to seek the support of any senior French soldier or diplomat who might be willing to return to Britain and lead the nation. Among them were Reynaud, Weygand, Lebrun, and former prime minister Leon Blum. There were numerous men with political standing who might have stepped forward to accept the challenge. For various reasons, none did.

The spacious flying boat, with room for more than 30 passengers, which Churchill had provided to fly French leaders to Britain departed virtually empty. Some Frenchmen had invoked the flimsy prospect that a resistance government might still take root in North Africa. Indeed, on Friday, June 21, the liner *Massilia* was released by Admiral of the Fleet and de facto commander of the entire French navy, Francois Darlan, and set sail for Casablanca. Chief among the passengers was former prime minister Daladier, and those aboard may well have believed that they were headed to North Africa to continue the fight.

Meanwhile, the drama of capitulation played out in the forest of Compiegne. Hitler and the Nazis had seen fit to exact their retribution for the armistice of November 1918, which had ended World War I, with a spectacle to humiliate the representatives of Pétain and the entire French nation. The old railroad car in which the Germans had signed the earlier armistice was brought from a museum in Paris, and the French delegation was led to it in the same place where the signing had occurred nearly a quarter century earlier.

Hitler denied Mussolini's request that Italy be awarded territory including the port cities of Toulon and Marseilles, the valley of the River Rhone, and dominion over Corsica, Tunisia, and Djibouti, a city in the horn of Africa that was adjacent to Italian-held Ethiopia. Instead, the Führer had opted to present the French with 23 conditions for the end of hostilities, none of which, he hoped, would induce them to continue armed resistance.

Intending to separate France from Britain, Hitler sought to "secure, if possible, a French government functioning on French territory. This would be far preferable to a situation in which the French might reject the German proposals and flee abroad to London to continue the war from there."[4]

While the British had been rightly concerned with the disposition of the French Fleet, and Churchill had been repeatedly assured that it would not be surrendered to the Germans, Hitler had conversely determined that the fleet should not fall into British hands. In order to assuage any French concern on this point, he offered a dubious assurance to the delegation in the surrender terms. "The German government solemnly declares to the French government that it does not intend to use for its own purposes in the war the French fleet which is in ports under German supervision.... Furthermore, they solemnly and expressly declare that they have no intention of raising any claim to the French fleet at the time of conclusion of peace."[5]

At 7 p.m. on June 22, General Huntziger signed the armistice agreement on behalf of the Pétain government. When they heard that the armistice had been concluded, those French officials aboard the *Massilia* en route to Casablanca attempted to persuade the captain of the vessel to change course and sail for Britain. However, the request was refused. When the ship arrived in North Africa, its passengers were placed under arrest and confined to the ship in the harbor.

In London, a politically astute de Gaulle moved to establish himself as either the legitimate leader of the French resistance or as a willing subordinate to the authority of a more senior officer or diplomat.

Debate continues as to his actual motivation. Regardless, he did send a telegram to the headquarters of General Auguste Nogues, in Rabat, Morocco, on June 19 stating, "Hold myself at your disposal, whether to fight under your orders or for any step which might seem to you useful."

Nogues, the commander of French forces in North Africa, had expressed a sentiment to resist the Nazis but abruptly changed course when the armistice was signed, as evidenced by his request for instructions on dealing with the diplomats aboard the *Massilia*. Curiously, he maintained a degree of independence under the Vichy government and kept his Moroccan troops, the fierce Goums, armed and under his personal control. Eventually, these troops were released to Allied command and fought with distinction in Italy. On this occasion, however, de Gaulle received no reply of substance.

Further, on June 20 de Gaulle appears to have parted with his standard course of action and swallowed his pride in a personal letter written to Weygand, whom he detested. "I feel that it is my duty to tell you quite simply that I do wish for the sake of France and for yours that you may be willing to remove yourself from disaster, reach colonial France and continue the war. At this time, there is no possible armistice with honor. I could be of use to you or to any other prominent Frenchman who is willing to place himself in command of a continued French resistance movement."

The letter, which was sent to Weygand through the French military attaché in London, was returned to de Gaulle three months after it was written. Along with it was a note that advised the sender to communicate with Weygand through appropriate government or military channels.

With the outward appearance of a willingness to be led, Charles de Gaulle had invited another individual, someone better known and possibly better received by the governments of Great Britain and the United States, and more important, someone to whom the armed forces of the far-flung empire would rally, to come forward and assume the role of leader of the resistance. One tantalizing question lingers. How would he have reacted if a notable Frenchman had done just that?

As it was, shock and paralysis gripped the diplomatic and military leadership of France. As Pétain capitulated and the Vichy regime was born, not a single person came forward to contest de Gaulle for the role he had always believed himself destined to play.

As he had promised, he took to the BBC microphone again on Wednesday, June 19. This time, his tone was much more emphatic. "Faced by the bewilderment of my countrymen," he said,

> by the disintegration of a government in thrall to the enemy, by the fact that the institutions of my country are incapable, at the moment, of functioning, I, General de Gaulle, a French soldier and military leader, realize that I now speak for France.
>
> In the name of France, I make the following solemn declaration: It is the bounden duty of all Frenchmen who still bear arms to continue the struggle. For them to lay down their arms, to evacuate any position of military importance, or to agree to hand over any part of French territory, however small, would be a crime against our country.... Soldiers of France, wherever you may be, arise![6]

This second appeal was delivered while Monnet was in Bordeaux on his last-ditch British-sponsored mission to find a prominent Frenchman to come to London. Apparently, de Gaulle was also keenly aware of his opportunity to move while Monnet was absent. Although the two had been cordial, they disagreed on the method and the means by which to shape a cohesive French resistance to the Nazis.

Monnet saw events as moving too rapidly and was concerned that de Gaulle's declaration that he represented the country might alienate the leadership of the French empire across the globe. Such a situation would only make matters of resistance more difficult. He also believed that any resistance movement organized and centered in London would look to all the world as a puppet of the British government.

For de Gaulle, the moment to act was at hand. His intense nationalism trumped the perceived need for consensus among Frenchmen outside the immediate reach of the Pétain government. Monnet later chose not to join de Gaulle and the Free French, but accepted an appointment by the British government to work with its purchasing mission in Washington, DC.

When news of the armistice reached London, there was undoubtedly a final acknowledgment that a resistance movement was the best hope for Frenchmen to continue fighting. On June 23, the British government issued two landmark statements. The first condemned the separate peace, and the second, without specifically naming de Gaulle, expressed its intent to work with French leaders in exile.

"The Armistice which has just been signed, in violation of the agreement solemnly concluded between the allied governments, places the Bordeaux government in a state of total subjection to the enemy, depriving it of all freedom and of any right to represent free French citizens. Consequently, His Majesty's government no longer considers the government of Bordeaux as that of an independent country," read the initial communiqué. This was followed by the announcement that Britain had become aware of a "plan for the formation of a provisional French National Committee" that would represent those "independent French elements resolved to fulfill the international obligations contracted by France" and that it "would recognize... [and] discuss with it all matters connected with the prosecution of the war."[7]

Of course, the head of this French National Committee was to be Charles de Gaulle, who was given as office space the third floor of the St. Stephen's House along the bank of the river Thames and near the House of Commons. There was to be an oath—to serve this newly and largely self-appointed leader with honor, fidelity, and discipline. A number of French government officials shied away, including Corbin, who chose retirement in South America rather than partnership with the Free French, as the committee soon came to be known. Those who chose early to enlist with de Gaulle occupied offices near their leader, on the third floor of a somewhat dingy building in a foreign country.

By June 26, any ambiguity as to the British position with regard to the Free French and its de facto leader was erased. A British diplomatic mission to Morocco had been rebuffed, and Churchill called de Gaulle to his quarters at 10 Downing Street. "You are all alone," said the prime minister. "Well then, I recognize you all alone." This was followed by a declaration that "recognizes General de Gaulle as leader of all the Free French, wherever they may be who join him in the defense of the Allied cause." Although this aroused some protest within the government, it was at long last done. In an evening radio address, de Gaulle stated boldly, "I take under my authority all the French who are now living in British territory or who may arrive later."

Setting about the business of government—or something similar to government—posed great challenges for the fledgling Free French. The 100,000 francs contributed by Reynaud were exchanged for only 100 pounds sterling, a paltry treasury at best. Diplomatic relations with the British were entrusted to Gaston Palewski, who had been personally summoned to London from Tunisia. As for the military, remnants of French army units were scattered in London and southern England, some of which had been ferried to safety from the debacle at Dunkirk.

Altogether, about 20,000 French soldiers were in Britain, including the 13th Demi-brigade of the Foreign Legion, a light division of mountain troops, a few dozen pilots, and an odd collection of volunteers. Only a trickle of men came to the Free French recruiting station at Olympia Hall. A poster bearing the French Tricolor was printed, and the message was from the leader in exile. "To all Frenchmen," it read. "France has lost a battle, but France has not lost the war. Some chance-gathered authorities, giving way to panic and forgetting honor, may have surrendered, delivering the country over into bondage. Yet nothing is lost! That is why I call upon all Frenchmen, wherever they may be, to join me in action, in sacrifice and in hope."

Soon, the Free French adopted the Cross of Lorraine as their symbol. It was a reminder of the province of Lorraine, which had long been disputed territory and was now again under the control of the Germans. Perhaps even more powerfully, it reminded the French people of the emblem under which Saint Joan of Arc had fought an occupying enemy centuries earlier.

A division, which had been involved in an unsuccessful campaign in Norway, arrived as well. Its commander, General Émile Béthouart, was for a time the senior French army officer in Britain. He declined to join de Gaulle or to subordinate himself to his junior. Instead, he eventually made his way to North Africa and fought on, serving capably. Before he departed, Béthouart arranged for de Gaulle to address several units and enlist their support for the Free French cause. Following one address, de Gaulle was reportedly successful in persuading 1,000 men to join him. Nevertheless, the recruiting process was painfully slow.

One of Béthouart's junior officers, Captain André Dewavrin, sought the Free French headquarters on his own and finally reached St. Stephen's House after a confusing journey that had been all the more complicated because road signs had been removed or camouflaged. Courcel received the young officer and presented him to de Gaulle.

Years later, Dewavrin remembered the meeting:

I walked into a spacious well-lit room. Two large windows opened onto the Thames. The huge form unwound and stood up to greet me. [The General] made me repeat my name and then asked me a series of short questions in a clear, incisive, rather harsh tone:

"Are you on the active list or the reserve?"

"Active, sir."

"Passed staff college?"

"No."

"Where were you?"

"The École Polytechnique."

"What were you doing before the mobilization?"

"Professor of Fortification at the École Spéciale Militaire de Saint Cyr."

"Have you any other qualifications? Do you speak English?"

"I have a degree in law and I speak English fluently, sir."

"Where were you during the war?"

"With the expeditionary corps in Norway."

"Then you know Tissier (newly appointed chief of staff). Are you senior to him?"

"No, sir."

"Very well. You will be the head of the second and third bureau on my staff. Good day. I shall see you again soon."

The conversation was over. I saluted and went out. The reception had been glacial.[8]

The Vichy government did not sit idly by while the spectacular Free French affront developed. By the end of the month, de Gaulle's temporary rank of general had been rescinded, he had been forced into retirement and summarily stripped of his French citizenship, and a message delivered through the French embassy in London ordered him to report to prison in Toulouse within five days in preparation for trial on charges of disobedience. This tribunal found him guilty, sentenced him to four years in prison, and levied a fine of one hundred francs.

In a second trial held in early July, he was found guilty of desertion and undertaking to serve a foreign country. This tribunal voted five to two to convict and sentenced him to death in absentia. Although Pétain voiced his agreement with this verdict and the sentence, he was reported by some to have vowed that the death sentence would never be carried out.

De Gaulle responded to the events at Vichy with disdain, saying that he considered its actions null and void and that he would have a discussion after the war with those who pronounced his guilt and his sentence. Only de Gaulle could actually grasp the potential personal consequences of the path he had chosen; however, it was not time to count the cost. There was a swirl of activity and business at hand.

Meanwhile, Yvonne had reached London and eventually decided to relocate to an unpretentious home outside the city. Charles would commute via Victoria Station on those occasions when he was able to see his family.

Even as efforts to establish the Free French organization were bearing some fruit, events occurred that nearly stopped the progress in its tracks. The Vichy government had already reneged on its pledge to transfer captured German airmen to British custody in order to prevent their taking part in the coming Battle of Britain, and indeed these pilots and crewmen were active once again with the Luftwaffe. The disposition of the French Fleet remained an open question, and Darlan, commander of the Vichy armed forces, was not to be trusted.

Churchill decided to take action to maintain the preeminence of the Royal Navy, particularly in the Mediterranean. Elements of the French fleet were already in the British ports of Plymouth and Portsmouth, and these were seized on the morning of July 3, with Royal Navy and Marine boarding parties taking control and marching the French crews to internment. Four British participants were wounded, and a French sailor was killed. A total of 130 French vessels were taken under British control.

Other French warships were under either German or Vichy control at Cherbourg, Toulon, and Brest, or scattered in North African ports. The most substantial concentration of French naval assets was located at the port of Mers el-Kébir, in Algeria. These included the battleships *Strasbourg, Dunkerque, Bretagne,* and *Provence,* six destroyers, and a complement of support vessels and submarines.

Churchill ordered Admiral Sir James Somerville to sail from Gibraltar with an ultimatum for the French commander, Admiral Marcel Gensoul. The French could sail with the Royal Navy warships and continue to resist the Germans; sail to British ports with reduced crews, tender their ships, and be repatriated to France; or sail to the island of Martinique in the West Indies, where they would be disarmed and out of the reach of the Germans.

Somerville, whose Force H consisted of the battleships *Valiant* and *Resolution,* the battlecruiser *Hood,* the aircraft carrier *Ark Royal,* and several cruisers and destroyers, reached the French anchorage on July 3 with firm instructions from Churchill to conclude the difficult task by the end of the day. A British destroyer entered the harbor and delivered the message to Gensoul. Its conclusion was ominous should the French choose not to comply with one of the three options offered: "We must with profound regret require you to sink your ships within six hours or it is the orders of His Majesty's government to use whatever force may be necessary to prevent your ships from falling into German or Italian hands."

Gensoul, who took his orders from Darlan, rejected the ultimatum, and just before 6 p.m. the British opened fire on the anchored French ships. Only the *Strasbourg* and an escorting destroyer managed to raise steam and escape from the carnage. Nearly 1,300 French sailors were killed and more than 350 wounded. It was a moment of supreme and tragic irony, in which the defenders of freedom had come to blows and the oppressors would find fodder for their propaganda machine.

Churchill regretted the decision to fire on the French but considered it a necessity. He later wrote, "Here was Britain, who so many had considered down and out, which strangers had supposed to be quivering on the brink of surrender to the mighty power arrayed against her, striking ruthlessly at her dearest friends of yesterday and securing for a while to herself the undisputed command of the sea.

It was made plain that the British War Cabinet feared nothing and would stop at nothing."

De Gaulle received word of the Mers el-Kébir tragedy on the evening of June 3 and erupted in both anger and anguish. As the leader of the Free French movement, supported by Great Britain, he appeared at worst to have potentially been a party to the terrible event. At best, it was those on whom he depended who had placed his entire effort in jeopardy. Recruiting to the cause would only be more difficult, and even more troublesome, he would be required to speak to the situation on the BBC. Prolonged silence would be unacceptable. He would gather himself and do what was necessary.

Churchill, at times a harsh political realist, understood the precarious position in which the action at Mers el-Kébir had placed de Gaulle and invited the Frenchman to lunch at 10 Downing Street. Together with Mrs. Churchill he conversed with de Gaulle, and inevitably the discussion turned to the unfortunate situation. Fluent in French, Mrs. Churchill expressed a hope that the navies of the two countries might yet work together. De Gaulle responded that the French Fleet might gain its greatest satisfaction by actually turning its guns on the British.

When Mrs. Churchill replied in perfect French that the remark was unbecoming for an ally or guest of Great Britain, the prime minister intervened and attempted to settle the conversation down. However, Mrs. Churchill persisted and stated, "No Winston, it is because there are certain things that a woman can say to a man which a man cannot say, and I am saying them to you, General de Gaulle."

Taken aback, de Gaulle, for one of the few times in his life, apologized to Mrs. Churchill and sent a large basket of flowers to her the following day. The general and the lady remained friendly from that time on, and it was said that she was an advocate for him with her husband whenever possible.[9]

On July 8, a resolute de Gaulle took to the radio once again. His higher calling had not diminished the sorrow and frustration of Mers el-Kébir, but somehow he knew that it was bound to happen. Perhaps on that evening he displayed his finest diplomatic ability of the entire war.

"Though seeing this tragedy as what it is, I mean as lamentable and hateful, Frenchmen worthy of the name cannot be unaware that the defeat of England would confirm their bondage forever. Our two ancient nations, our two great nations remain bound to one another. They will either go down both together or both together they will win."

As horrific as Mers el-Kébir had been, it served to strengthen the bond between the Free French movement and Great Britain, and certainly the personal ties between Churchill and de Gaulle. Despite the fact that the Vichy government would use Mers el-Kébir as a propaganda weapon, it also severed political ties with Great Britain, a development that further legitimized and strengthened de Gaulle's authority. He had contemplated giving up and relocating to a quiet life in Canada, but only momentarily. Capable of comprehending the noble purpose that lay ahead, de Gaulle chose leadership and vision rather than a base, reactionary response. Therein lay the foundation of greatness.

Within weeks of the appointment of Free French staff officials, agents were secretly sent to France to contact those pledged to resist the occupiers from within. A coordinated resistance, embryonic though it was, began to take shape. On Bastille Day, July 14, 1940, the Free French, such as they were, gathered in Grosvenor Gardens. There were actually more British than French in attendance, but all joined in a rendition of the *Marseillaise,* the French national anthem. The moment bolstered de Gaulle's confidence that he had won the admiration of the British people. To many of them, he stood out as the only Frenchman willing to continue an armed resistance against the Nazis, the only man who would work to restore his country's honor, and the only man who understood the solemn pledge his nation had made to fight side by side with Britain to the end.

While the Vichy government might posture and pronounce, its reach would prove limited. Its soon to be vilified collaborationist prime minister Pierre Laval might push for even greater cooperation with the Nazis, but with each passing day the prospect of a quick British surrender became less likely. It was to vanish altogether with the Battle of Britain. Further, the will to resist was revived in the French empire. The distant New Hebrides had declared an allegiance to the Free French by the end of June. The governor of Chad, Félix Éboué, pledged his support as well. There were also stirrings in the French Congo. Emissaries were dispatched to secure these colonies.

By August, the Free French and the British government had concluded an agreement for continuing cooperation, including the financing of the Free French movement with the equivalent of $40 million from the British treasury.

De Gaulle had also sought guarantees from the British for the restoration of France and its empire, control over the Free French armed forces that he was actively recruiting, and an understanding that French soldiers fighting under the command of British officers would not be required to fight other Frenchmen. Churchill was in no position to fully guarantee these points. After all, the outcome of the war was far from certain. Britain's own colonial empire was at risk, and a guarantee of French colonial possessions was quite a stretch. As for Frenchmen fighting Frenchmen, the question would sort itself out should Free French soldiers confront those of Vichy on the battlefield.

While he did not achieve the full measure of his requests, de Gaulle had successfully solidified his hold on the leadership of Frenchmen in exile. The British would deal with him. He would shape the future course of French resistance.

With the heroic defense of the skies over Britain ongoing, Churchill was on the offensive. Hitting the Germans by some means was attractive, and involving the forces of the Free French might enhance the movement's prestige around the world. At the western tip of the continent of Africa was the port city of Dakar, which had been a French possession since 1857. Although strong-willed pro-Vichy governor Pierre Boisson was in firm control, a joint military operation involving British and Free French troops might succeed in capturing the port, hopefully without bloodshed, and could bring all of French West Africa into the Allied sphere. From the beginning, de Gaulle had misgivings about such an operation, acknowledging that Dakar might be strongly defended. However, he decided to move forward believing that if he did not act the British might do so on their own in the future to prevent Dakar from becoming a haven for German U-boats operating in the Atlantic.

In late September, a naval task force arrived off Dakar with de Gaulle himself aboard one of the ships and 2,500 Free French troops and two battalions of Royal Marines poised to land. Boisson, however, was resolute. Appeals for peaceful cooperation were flatly rejected, and Free French sympathizers in Dakar had already been rounded up and jailed. Under a flag of truce, de Gaulle approached the shore only to be informed that an order for his arrest had been issued. An argument ensued, and it became apparent that no progress would be made. As the Free French delegation backed out of the harbor, machine guns opened fire and injured at least one person.

Fog hampered the operations of Royal Navy warships, which exchanged gunfire with the French battleship *Richelieu* moored in the harbor. An attempted landing was aborted when the escorting Free French warship was hit by fire from shore batteries. To make matters worse, a Vichy submarine slipped from the harbor and slammed a torpedo into the British battleship *Resolution*. At last, the invasion force was compelled to withdraw to Freetown in the British colony of Sierra Leone. The entire adventure had ended in failure and colossal embarrassment for Churchill. Most of the blame, though, fell unjustly on the shoulders of de Gaulle.

Although postwar German naval records confirmed that neither Vichy nor German authorities had been aware of the Dakar operation ahead of time, rumors of security breaches among the Free French were rampant. It followed that de Gaulle and company might not be trustworthy or even capable of cooperating in any future military endeavor. Doubtless, Dakar was the low point of the Free French movement.

Churchill defended de Gaulle to the best of his ability and told the House of Commons that mistakes had been made at Dakar. De Gaulle, despondent over the failure, contemplated suicide. Nevertheless, the Allied reception elsewhere in equatorial Africa was more enthusiastic. During the coming weeks, de Gaulle traveled through the French colonial possessions in the region. Aware that the British and Vichy governments were in contact with one another through diplomatic channels, this was a bold step that reached beyond the scope of de Gaulle's understanding with the British government. It also rattled the British Foreign Office, which had hoped to keep Vichy from completely changing sides and entering the war as an Axis minion.

Continuing his efforts to rally support for the Free French movement among France's colonies, de Gaulle imperiled his tenuous relationship with the British government. He asserted control that had been granted by no real authority. De Gaulle was filling a power vacuum with decisive, rapid, and independent action.

On October 27, 1940, at Brazzaville, in the French Congo, de Gaulle issued a declaration announcing the formation of a Defense Council of the Empire, which was tantamount to the establishment of a dictatorial government of French possessions, and asserted, "Decisions will be taken by the leader of the Free French, after consultation, if the need arises, with the Defense Council." A few days later, a second communiqué declared that the government of Pétain was unlawful. De Gaulle had not consulted with the British prior to issuing the declaration, and to compound the difficulty he contacted the US consulate at Leopoldville in the Belgian Congo, hoping to open a discussion of the administration of French colonies in the western hemisphere.

While it was true that more and more of colonial France and well-known officers in the French military were rallying to the Free French, it was also apparent that de Gaulle was quickly tiring of simply being the head of a national committee backed by the British. His was to be a government with full diplomatic standing and recognition among nations. For their part, the Americans were not at war in the autumn of 1940 and had little interest in de Gaulle or the Free French. In their estimation, the Vichy government was the government of France. Dakar had done nothing to change their opinion, and now the upstart de Gaulle had the audacity to communicate as a head of state. There is no record of a reply from the US State Department.

De Gaulle returned to London on November 12, following a rather curt communication from Churchill, which read in part, "I feel most anxious for consultation with you. Situation between France and Britain has changed remarkably since you left.... We have hopes of Weygand in Africa and no one must underrate advantage that would follow if he were to be rallied. We are trying to arrive at some modus vivendi with Vichy which would minimize the risk of incidents and will enable some favorable forces in France to develop.... You will see how important it is that you should be here."[10]

Since the debacle of Dakar in September, Charles de Gaulle had no doubt been keenly aware of the danger that existed. For as much as the Free French might need the British, an overture from Vichy or the rise to greater prominence of someone of stature, such as Weygand, who had in fact been sent by Pétain to assume the post of Delegate General of the French North African colonies, could prove his undoing.

Therefore, his action at Brazzaville is understandable. The growth of the Free France movement with the pledge of allegiance from possessions in the Pacific, the Indian subcontinent, and equatorial Africa would make any deal that excluded de Gaulle from a prominent place at the table more difficult. De Gaulle also realized that he needed the

British but remained wary of both Churchill's government and the Americans throughout the war years and beyond.

In the mid-1950s, he wrote in his memoirs,

> To start with...I was nothing. Not the semblance of a force or an organization was behind me....But my very poverty showed me the line to take....Only if I acted as the inflexible champion of the nation and the state could I win support among the French and respect from foreigners. The critics who persisted in frowning on my intransigence refused to see that I was controlling countless conflicting pressures and that the least yielding would have led to total collapse. Precisely because I was alone and without power I had to climb the peaks and never afterwards descend from that level.[11]

Constantly intending to prove that he was no puppet of the British, de Gaulle clashed with his hosts over military and diplomatic issues in the Middle East, quelled dissent against his course of action and rivalry among the members of his own national committee, and managed to stir the anger of even his closest friends in the British government. During one sharp exchange with his liaison officer, General Spears, he spewed venom. "I do not believe that I will ever get along with the English. You are all the same, absorbed in your own interests and business, and very insensitive to the requirements of others. You believe that I am interested in England winning the war? I am not! I am only interested in the victory of France."[12]

From 1941 on, the relationship between the Free French and the British and American governments was one of wary suspicion. The strained relationship was heightened when America entered the war in December of that year.

During the summer of 1941, British and Free French troops fought side by side in a successful campaign to secure Syria and Lebanon from pro-Axis regimes and potential occupation by the Germans. Meanwhile, however, terms were concluded with the Vichy forces in the Levant by British military commanders who did not fully appreciate the delicate nature of Anglo-Free French relations. The interests of the Free French were virtually dismissed. An amended agreement was signed and a crisis averted. Again, the hand of de Gaulle had been inflexible, and his policy of intransigence had paid a dividend.

There were other rifts between Churchill and de Gaulle, not the least of which had to do with an interview the Free French leader granted to George Weller, a reporter for the *Chicago Daily News*. In the published article, de Gaulle criticized the British.

"England is afraid of the French fleet," Weller quoted.

> What in effect England is carrying on is a wartime deal with Hitler in which Vichy serves as a go-between. Vichy serves Hitler in keeping the French people in subjection and selling the French empire piecemeal to Germany. But do not forget that Vichy also serves England by keeping the French fleet from Hitler's hands. Britain is exploiting Vichy the same way as Germany, the only difference is in purpose. What happens is in effect an exchange of advantages between hostile powers which keeps the Vichy government alive as long as both Britain and Germany are agreed that it should exist.[13]

Churchill fumed and refused to see de Gaulle until he had sufficiently cooled off. During a subsequent meeting, the prime minister warned the Frenchman that he should be careful in cultivating concerns that he was anti-British. Such was the nature of the tempestuous relationship.

Three weeks after Pearl Harbor, de Gaulle also wrangled with the US government over the tiny islands of St. Pierre and Miquelon, off the coast of Newfoundland. Concerns had arisen as to the possibility of weather equipment transmitting information that might be useful to the Germans. While the islands were French possessions, the United States objected to Free French forces from Halifax, Nova Scotia, occupying them. Instead, the Americans had agreed to a Canadian operation. When de Gaulle was informed, he ordered his small force to the islands ahead of the Canadians. The hostile US response was soothed by Churchill, who worked out a compromise allowing the parties at odds to save face. Still, de Gaulle had done little to endear himself to the Americans.

Since their early communications with the British government and their ongoing effort to support Weygand in North Africa were seen as the best hope to keep Vichy out of the war, the American government was reluctant to vest de Gaulle with any specific endorsement of substance. In the autumn of 1941, Free French representative René Pleven had traveled to Washington, DC, and requested a meeting with Roosevelt or Secretary of State Cordell Hull. Neither would receive him. The reception from Undersecretary of State Sumner Welles was icy.

After US entry into the war, the Roosevelt administration assumed a somewhat more pragmatic approach to de Gaulle and on July 9, 1942, issued a statement that affirmed the contribution of the Free French movement to the war effort and pledged military and humanitarian aid. The US maintained the stance that the French people should be allowed to freely elect their governing officials after the war. Whether de Gaulle would play a role in the postwar government was for the French voter to decide.

As the war continued, Free French forces fought with distinction in the desert at Bir Hacheim and elsewhere, participated in the abortive Commando raid on the French port city of Dieppe, and supported covert resistance operations inside the Vichy-controlled region of France, which the Germans occupied on November 11, 1942, following the Allied landings on the coast of North Africa three days earlier.

Operation Torch, as the landings were code-named, involved the first offensive action of American troops on the ground during the war against Nazi Germany. US and British landings were to occur on the North African coast at the major cities of Casablanca, Oran, and Algiers. It was hoped that the Vichy forces in control in these areas would quickly surrender and potentially rally to the Allied cause. The long-term goal was to crush German forces under Field Marshal Erwin Rommel between the British Eighth Army, which was advancing westward from the Egyptian frontier under General Bernard Law Montgomery following its victory at El Alamein, and the Americans in the west.

Although the Americans had initially pushed for an assault on the European continent, British military planners prevailed, and it was decided in July 1942 that French North Africa would be the location of the Allied offensive. However, there can be no doubt that Churchill otherwise accepted that the center of Allied power had shifted from London to Washington, DC, when the United States entered the war. The continuing mistrust of de Gaulle by the Roosevelt administration contributed mightily to a concerted effort to marginalize Free France, or Fighting France, as the movement had been renamed in June.

Hitler had launched his invasion of the Soviet Union on June 22, 1941, and during subsequent discussions with Soviet officials de Gaulle had promised to urge the opening of a second front in Europe as soon as possible. However, when Roosevelt and Churchill made their decision for North Africa, they also concluded that the Free French were not to be consulted, their aid would not be solicited, and above all, de Gaulle was to know nothing of Operation Torch.

By the summer of 1942, relations between Churchill and de Gaulle reached another low point. British troops had landed on the island of Madagascar, off the coast of East Africa, two months earlier, and de Gaulle had not been made aware of the operation even though he had proposed a joint effort to capture the island as early as December 1941. Perhaps the most adversarial meeting of their careers occurred at 10 Downing Street in September, and both men were smarting from its bitter conclusion, with Churchill even threatening to abandon de Gaulle in favor of another more agreeable French leader.

At the same time, the Roosevelt administration had embarked, with Churchill's quiet agreement, on a course to identify another prominent Frenchman who might supersede de Gaulle as the leader of the Free French. Further overtures to Weygand were thwarted when the general voiced his lasting allegiance to Pétain and evaporated when the Germans demanded his recall to France following the Torch landings.

The Americans then settled on General Henri Giraud, under whom de Gaulle had served at Metz in 1938. Giraud had escaped from a German prison and made his way to Vichy, where he declared his support for Pétain in glowing terms. Giraud was contacted by Allied agents, and heated negotiations ensued, with Giraud finally withdrawing his demand that he be placed in command of all Allied forces landing in North Africa. He agreed to command only French troops and to attempt to halt any Vichy resistance to the Torch landings. In exchange, he would be named governor general of North Africa.

It turned out that Giraud was every bit as difficult to deal with as de Gaulle might have been. To complicate matters, Admiral Darlan, commander of all Vichy armed forces, was coincidentally in Algiers on the day of the Torch landings. He had visited his son, who was suffering from polio, and his presence there did trump, to a great extent, any authority Giraud might attempt to exert over Vichy forces.

De Gaulle, meanwhile, had been made aware as early as August that something was afoot in North Africa. That warning may have come from the Soviets, who formally recognized the French National Committee as the "executive body" of Fighting France with the authority to organize French participation in the war.

On the morning of November 8, de Gaulle was awakened in London to the news of the Torch landings. "I hope the Vichy people will fling them into the sea! You can't break into France and get away with it!" he snarled.[14]

It fell to Churchill to brief the Fighting French leader on what was taking place, and by the time of their lunch appointment at Chequers, de Gaulle had cooled down a bit. In his memoirs, he recalled Churchill explaining, "We were forced to accept it. You can be sure that we are not in any way renouncing our agreements with you. As the business takes on its full extension, we British are to come into action. Then we shall have our word to say. It will be to support you. You were with us during the worst moments of the war. We shall not abandon you when the horizon clears."[15]

De Gaulle explained in a meeting with the National Committee that Churchill assured him that Giraud would play only a military role; however, it cannot be fully accepted that the politically astute de Gaulle was willing to simply take Churchill at his word. The Americans were running this show, and their man was Giraud. The days ahead might find de Gaulle without standing, and he knew it.

When he took to the BBC microphone on the evening of November 8, 1942, de Gaulle had completely changed his tune from the anger of the morning. It was evident that the liberation of France had begun with this offensive in North Africa. His comments were both reflective of his conviction that the future still held a prominent role for him and of the fact that the rank and file of the Fighting French and the French people as a whole needed a leader to stand firm.

"The Allies of France have undertaken to draw French North Africa into the war of liberation," he remarked.

> They are beginning to land enormous forces there. It is a question of so ordering matters that our Algeria, our Morocco and our Tunisia form the base, the beginning point for the liberation of France. Our American allies are at the head of this enterprise.
>
> The moment is very well chosen. Our British allies, seconded by the French troops, have just expelled the Germans and Italians from Egypt and they are making their way into Cyrenaica. Our Russian allies have definitively broken the enemy's supreme offensive. The

French people, gathered together in resistance, are only waiting for the moment to rise up as a whole. So French leaders, soldiers, sailors, airmen, officials, and colonists rise up now! Help our allies!

Come! The great moment is here. This is the time for common sense and courage. Everywhere the enemy is staggering and giving way. Frenchmen of North Africa, let us, through you, return to action from one end of the Mediterranean to the other. Then, the war will be won, and won thanks to France.[16]

The Allied landings in North Africa were met with varying degrees of resistance, and after nearly three days of fighting negotiations with Vichy France's Admiral Darlan ended in a cease-fire. However, the deal brokered by General Mark Clark, chief of staff to General Dwight D. Eisenhower, the overall Allied commander, raised a considerable degree of ire. Darlan was to be installed as the High Commissioner of France for North and West Africa with Giraud as his military commander.

Eisenhower had seen what was coming and told his senior commanders that he would accept responsibility for the political fallout that was certain to follow. Darlan was mistrusted and had commanded Vichy forces that had fired upon Allied troops—not to mention that de Gaulle was to once again be left out of the political picture. The Darlan fiasco hung like a cloud over the Allied governments, and sharp criticism was raised from every quarter. Although his motive remains unclear, a young assassin, Fernand Bonnier de La Chapelle, shot Darlan twice as he entered his office on December 24, killing him and removing a major embarrassment.

Darlan's body was barely cold when Giraud was installed as civil and military commander in French North Africa. Immediately, de Gaulle began to push for a meeting of the two French leaders to discuss the future. However, while Giraud delayed, Churchill and Roosevelt decided to meet at Casablanca and invited both Frenchmen to join them. When de Gaulle declined, Churchill twisted his arm, threatening to cut off financial support of the French National Committee if he refused. When he did come to Casablanca, Giraud had already been present there for five days. Roosevelt chided Churchill that he had been able to produce the bridegroom, Giraud, but that Churchill was having difficulty coaxing the bride, de Gaulle, to the altar. When the conference was over, there had been no shotgun wedding.

De Gaulle arrived on January 22 and was presented with a proposal that a council be formed with Giraud, de Gaulle and General Alphonse Georges, a prominent officer in North Africa who had refused to swear allegiance to Vichy, serving as copresidents. The council would include old Vichy enemies of de Gaulle, including Nogues and Boisson, who had resisted at Dakar and during the Torch landings. De Gaulle refused such a proposal, which would in effect have given Free France over to Giraud, the vassal of Britain and the United States.

In an attempt to salvage something, Roosevelt asked de Gaulle if he would at least agree to be photographed shaking hands with Giraud. When the shutter clicked, one of the more famous images of World War II was preserved, and the look of disdain on de Gaulle's face is readily apparent. Subsequently, the two Frenchmen did agree to exchange liaison officers.

For de Gaulle, the meeting at Casablanca had been an exercise in personal resolve. He had refused to buckle under pressure from Roosevelt and Churchill, and he had won a foothold in North Africa. In reference to Giraud, he had measured the man. During the months to follow, Giraud would prove no match for the politically savvy de Gaulle.

By March, support for Giraud among the population of North Africa and within the French National Committee had eroded substantially, and when he cabled de Gaulle to request a meeting to discuss a unified French leadership it was de Gaulle who advised that the proposal of a copresidency put forward at Casablanca was as dead as Darlan. Early 1943 marked the rising tide of Charles de Gaulle. The resistance movement within France had grown steadily under the leadership of Jean Moulin, and when the two conferred in London in February plans were set in motion to convene the National Council of the Resistance, pledged to the support of the Free French.

Just as heartening, the Germans and Italians were expelled from the continent of North Africa in May, and the Frenchmen under arms there numbered 450,000. The Free French units there had actively participated in the fighting and were well respected for their contribution to the victory. Thus, the leader of Free France was well positioned to come to North Africa on his own terms rather than being summoned by another individual of greater perceived stature.

Churchill was still under pressure from Washington to dump de Gaulle, and the prime minister was still smarting from the intransigence of the Frenchman at Casablanca. The extent of his exasperation was such that he confined de Gaulle to London, restricted his access to the BBC, and even requested that the War Cabinet sanction a break with the French National Committee as long as de Gaulle was at its head. The request was denied, and it was plain to most observers who were close to the situation that time was running out for Giraud.

Roosevelt, too, had been vexed by the stubborn de Gaulle. In mid-May, he cabled Churchill the following:

"I am fed up with de Gaulle and the secret personal and political machinations of that committee in the last few days indicates that there is no possibility of our working with him. I am absolutely convinced that he has been and is now injuring our war effort and that he is a very dangerous threat to us. The time has arrived when we must break with him. It is an intolerable situation. We must have someone whom we can completely and wholly trust."[17]

Roosevelt was continually astounded that de Gaulle could assert any authority whatsoever. His country had been conquered. He had depended on the goodwill of others. France had lost control of its own destiny. The government at Vichy represented Roosevelt's idea of France—a nation that had capitulated and was to be rescued by the force of Allied arms.

Roosevelt saw de Gaulle as an impudent upstart who likened himself to the reincarnation of Joan of Arc and Clemenceau. The president's superficial view of France and French history failed to comprehend the depth of the philosophical differences between the Fighting French and the collaborationists at Vichy. For de Gaulle, each slight, each insult was not only taken personally but also as an insult to the French nation. He was unapologetic, refusing to bend a knee or to beg for anything.

In turn, Roosevelt believed that de Gaulle had committed a serious affront with the occupation of St. Pierre and Miquelon. The president often openly questioned de Gaulle's motivation, assessing the Fighting French leader as a would-be dictator and even a fascist sympathizer. Roosevelt did not trust de Gaulle, and the feeling was mutual. The president believed that the best approach to pressuring de Gaulle was through his British benefactors, and at times Churchill found himself caught between the rock of de Gaulle's obstinance and the hard place of Roosevelt's stubbornness.

Despite their recent wrangling, de Gaulle wrote to Churchill on May 27, 1943, "As I leave London for Algeria, where I am called by my difficult mission in the service of France, I look back over the long stage of nearly three years of war which Fighting France has accomplished side by side with Great Britain and based on British territory. I am more confident than ever in the victory of our two countries along with all their allies, and I am more convinced than ever that you personally will be the man of the days of glory, just as you were the man of the darkest hours."[18]

De Gaulle visited British Foreign Secretary Anthony Eden, who smiled and commented, "Do you know that you have caused us more difficulties than all our other European allies put together?" He smiled in response, saying, "I don't doubt it. France is a great power."[19]

The time had come for the headquarters of Free France to relocate to Algiers as de Gaulle set about consolidating power, leaving an outmaneuvered Giraud in his wake. In less than a week, the two announced the formation of a French Committee of National Liberation, with de Gaulle and Giraud as copresidents and a council of five others. However, when Giraud departed for a three-week visit to the United States de Gaulle attended parades and was received enthusiastically across French North Africa. With the Allied invasion of Sicily, he provided logistical support in Giraud's absence.

By the time Giraud returned, de Gaulle had convinced the committee that his original plan, with himself as the political head of the committee and Giraud as the military commander, was the proper course. De Gaulle would be the committee chairman, and the copresidency would survive in name only. All this was accomplished by the end of July 1943. By the autumn, de Gaulle had consolidated power and constructed the basis for a provisional government over which he intended to assume authority in France following victory over the Nazis.

While the political jockeying continued, Allied armies were advancing on all fronts. The liberation of Sicily was followed, in September 1943, by Allied landings at Salerno on the Italian mainland, and Mussolini had been deposed two months earlier. The Soviet Red Army had won its victory at Stalingrad and embarked on a great offensive surge that would carry it all the way to Berlin. In the West, Britain and the United States had been planning an invasion of the European continent for months.

During that summer of victory, Yvonne and Anne relocated from London to a villa in the hills above Algiers. De Gaulle's daughter Elizabeth worked in the office of the National Committee, while his son, Philippe, served with the Free French navy.

Just as he had been excluded from official planning and discussion for the North African operation, de Gaulle was only on the periphery of the negotiations with Italian authorities that concluded with that nation officially switching to the Allied side. In addition, plans were under way for a military government in France after the war, under the administration of Great Britain and the United States. For de Gaulle, the intent was plain. France was to have a secondary role in the postwar world. Even Stalin had stated previously that he attached little importance to the Fighting French, which did not represent a great power and were of no consequence to the Soviet Union.

True to form, Roosevelt blocked any detailed disclosure to de Gaulle of the plans for Operation Overlord, the D-day invasion, and it was not until de Gaulle arrived in London on June 4, 1944, to confer with Churchill that any part of the plan for the liberation of Western Europe was shared with him, including plans for the future of the French government.

De Gaulle had no interest in discussing some cooperative arrangement with the British and Americans for the administration and government of liberated France. His Fighting French were the government. On that point, he would never yield. He also wanted to ensure that French troops, particularly the 2nd Armored Division under General Jacques Leclerc, should be equipped and landed in France as soon as possible to play some significant role in the liberation of Paris.

"Why do you seem to think that I am required to put myself up to Roosevelt as a candidate for power in France," he told the prime minister. "The French government exists. I have nothing to ask of the United States of America, any more than I have of Great Britain."

Churchill responded with equal ardor, "And what about you? How do you expect us, the British, to adopt a position separated from that of the United States? We are going to liberate Europe, but it is because the Americans are with us to do so. Any time we have to choose between Europe and the open seas, we shall always be for the open seas. Every time I have to choose between you and Roosevelt, I shall always choose Roosevelt."[20]

Following the audience with Churchill, de Gaulle visited the headquarters of General Dwight D. Eisenhower, supreme Allied commander in Europe, and was shown the text of a radio message the general intended to deliver regarding a provisional government of France. De Gaulle rejected the statement out of hand, withheld the deployment of a cadre of French liaison officers that were to accompany the Allied invasion force, and did not participate in a joint declaration with representatives of other governments in exile in support of Overlord. Instead, he chose to address the French people alone on the BBC on the afternoon of June 6, 1944.

"The supreme battle has begun," he said in a measured tone. "It is the battle in France, and it is the battle of France. France is going to fight this battle furiously. She is going to conduct it in due order. The clear, the sacred duty of the sons of France, wherever they are and whoever they are, is to fight the enemy with all the means at their disposal.

"The orders given by the French government and by the French leaders it has named for that purpose are to be obeyed exactly. The actions we carry out in the enemy's rear are to be coordinated as closely as possible with those carried out at the same time by the Allied and French armies. Let none of those capable of action, either by arms or by destruction or by giving intelligence or by refusing to do work useful to the enemy, allow themselves to be made prisoner. Let them remove themselves beforehand from being seized and from being deported.

"The battle of France has begun. In the nation, the empire and the armies there is no longer anything but one single hope, the same for all. Behind the terribly heavy cloud of our blood and our tears here is the sun of our grandeur shining out once again."[21]

De Gaulle made no concessions. His intentions were clear, and during the spring of 1944 numerous governments chose to recognize the de facto leadership of France. Grudgingly, both Roosevelt and Churchill would come to the same conclusion. The leaders of

Great Britain and the United States fumed, considering de Gaulle a hindrance and distraction to the business at hand. However, it was apparent that de Gaulle's control of the French Resistance, his influence with the French forces in the field, and his popularity among the French people as a whole constituted a force with which to be reckoned. The headstrong Frenchman made plans to return to his homeland for the first time in four years.

CHAPTER 7

Triumphant Return

ON THE BLUSTERY MORNING OF JUNE 14, EIGHT DAYS AFTER THE
D-day landings, Charles de Gaulle boarded the French destroyer
Combattante, which slipped out of the harbor of Portsmouth and
made for the beaches of Normandy near Courseulles. When he had
departed France in 1940, he was unknown to the people. Since then,
they had heard his voice on the BBC. They had taken note of his
influence on the resistance—and they knew him as a leader.

Following a brief stop at the field headquarters of General
Montgomery, commander of Allied ground forces engaged in
Operation Overlord, de Gaulle's entourage proceeded to Bayeux, the
largest city in France to have been liberated at the time. Along the
route, the entourage overtook two French policemen. After he told
them who he was, the startled gendarmes were asked to proceed into

the town 15 minutes ahead of the general to alert the population. Clearly, de Gaulle was apprehensive. He need not have worried.

A short visit with the city's prefect was punctuated with questions concerning such matters as food supplies and bomb damage. As they left the city hall, one of de Gaulle's aides noticed a portrait of Marshal Pétain on the wall. Swiftly, it was removed. A new order had come to France. A crowd had gathered in the Place du Chateau, and soon there were cheers, bouquets, a brief address, and a loud rendition of the *Marseillaise* led by the general himself.

Years later, he wrote, "We walked through the streets. When the inhabitants realized that this was General de Gaulle, they gazed in silence at first—in a sort of stupor—then burst into cheers and tears. They came out of their houses and joined me, full of emotion. Children surrounded me, women smiled and sobbed, men shook my hand. We walked on like one family, overwhelmed with joy and pride, feeling the hope of our nation rise with us from the depths."[1]

Stops at Isigny and Grandcamp were equally well received, and the news media reported the triumphant but brief return to the rest of the world. Although Churchill remained exasperated and Roosevelt suspicious, the visit to the beachhead facilitated some improvement in de Gaulle's relations with the United States. For one thing, it did not appear that de Gaulle intended to return to France as a dictator imposing his will on the people. They had welcomed him as the defender of their honor and the individual who could safeguard the position of France among the great nations of the world. Whatever lingering doubt there may have been in de Gaulle's mind as to the legitimacy of his effort evaporated at Bayeux.

Although Roosevelt's personal opinion of de Gaulle did not change, he issued an invitation for the general to visit Washington. A previous such invitation had been refused months earlier; however, this one was accepted. De Gaulle later wrote in his memoirs, "The indications of French unity were now too clear for anyone to ignore.

The President of the United States at last acknowledged as much. I had no favors to ask, and I would undertake no negotiations. The conversations would have no other object than inquiry into worldwide problems of interest to both countries. If, afterward, the American government wanted to open negotiations with the French government about relations between the Allied armies and our administration it could do so, like the British government, through normal diplomatic channels."[2]

On July 12, 1944, the US government released a statement that de Gaulle and his national committee were qualified to exercise civil administration in liberated France. De Gaulle's administrators were taking control in the liberated areas, arresting collaborators, replacing local officials who had been too cozy with Vichy, and distributing their own paper currency to replace that provided by the British and US governments.

By mid-July, the pace of liberation had begun to quicken. Allied troops broke out of the Normandy hedgerows and into open country. A rapid dash across France would surely reach Paris within days. The capital city was the symbol of the nation, and it would be imperative for French troops to participate in its liberation. The provisional government would then be established in its rightful place. To the south, the Allied invasion of the French Mediterranean coast, Operation Dragoon, began on August 15 with landings in the vicinity of Saint-Tropez, Cavalaire-sur-mer, and Saint-Raphael. French commandos took part in the landings, destroying German artillery emplacements at Cap Negre, on the western edge of the landing beaches.

Still smarting from his difficult luncheon with Churchill weeks earlier, de Gaulle snubbed the prime minister, who had flown to Algiers to board a warship and observe the naval bombardment during the first day of Operation Dragoon. As Allied forces approached Paris, the general's distrust of both the British and Americans heightened. A series of unfortunate events occurred during de Gaulle's return to France in preparation for the liberation of the City of Light, aggravating his paranoia and conviction that some Anglo-American conspiracy was afoot.

On August 17, 1944, an American plane that was to transport the general to France overshot its runway and was disabled on landing. When he was informed that a second plane would fly to Casablanca to pick him up, de Gaulle boarded his personal Lockheed Lodestar for the flight to the coast of Morocco. Under British flight restrictions, the second American plane was required to land at Gibraltar. When it burst a tire and de Gaulle was informed that the necessary repairs would take 24 hours, he decided to continue aboard the Lodestar, which had also flown to Gibraltar with members of his staff, as soon as it could be made ready for departure.

De Gaulle disliked flying and chain-smoked during the last leg of the journey. An escort of Royal Air Force fighters could not be located in weather that was getting worse by the minute, and to compound problems the Lodestar's range would be stretched to its limit without refueling in Britain. When he was informed of the need to refuel, de Gaulle flatly refused, convinced that the conniving British authorities would find some excuse to delay his departure. Instead, the Lodestar flew on through the worsening weather as the fuel gauge hovered near empty.

When the coast of France was finally identified, the pilot was unsure of the location, and de Gaulle himself identified the contour of the land below as slightly east of the port of Cherbourg. The intended destination, an airfield at Maupertuis, was just out of reach, and the Lodestar landed at a small fighter strip. Thus, on August 20, following three days of mishaps, however accidental they may have been, Charles de Gaulle was in France once again.

The following day, he met with Eisenhower, who had planned to bypass Paris to the north and south. He reminded the general that the French capital was an important communications center and noted that a general uprising had been instigated by communist members of the resistance within the city. Of course, de Gaulle knew instinctively that the communist move was a direct threat to his authority and the provisional government that he would lead. Had Eisenhower refused to divert Leclerc's 2nd Armored Division to Paris, de Gaulle fully intended to send a formal letter to the Allied commander the following day, August 21, informing him that the leader of the French government would take direct control of the French division and order it to Paris himself.

In his wartime memoir *Crusade in Europe,* Eisenhower wrote, "In this matter my hand was forced by the action of the Free French forces inside Paris.... Information indicated that no great battle would take place and it was believed that the entry of one or two Allied divisions would accomplish the liberation of the city."

De Gaulle did in fact send his letter to Eisenhower, and the Supreme Allied Commander scrawled across it, "It looks now as if we'd be compelled to go into Paris. Bradley and his G-2 [General Omar Bradley, commander of the US Twelfth Army Group and his intelligence officer] think we can and must walk in."[3]

De Gaulle summoned Leclerc and other Free French leaders to the seventeenth-century chateau at Rambouillet on August 22, and briefed the small group on plans for the reentry into Paris. That evening, as he readied for an uneasy rest, he was ushered toward the suite where the kings and heads of state of France had slept during the past 150 years.

Taken aback, de Gaulle admonished his aide who had made the arrangements. He had no intention of sleeping in the same bed as those who had led the French government in the past. Symbolic though it was, this vignette is revealing of his intent to ultimately allow the French people to determine the leadership of the postwar government.

On the morning of August 25, 1944, Leclerc's troops and tanks rolled into the center of Paris. Four years of Nazi occupation were over. The German commander of the city's garrison, General Deitrich von Choltitz, who had disobeyed orders to destroy the city before Allied forces arrived, was taken into custody. Isolated pockets of Germans continued to fight, but the news of the liberation quickly spread, and the people of Paris took to the streets.

Charles de Gaulle was well aware of the importance of the occasion and of the impression that he should make on the resistance factions which might, in the wake of the Nazis, challenge his authority and plunge the nation into civil war. In his memoirs, he wrote of the thoughts that entered his mind during the drive from Rambouillet.

"I myself had already determined what I must do in the liberated capital," he remembered. "I would mold all minds into a single national impulse but also cause the figure and the authority of the state to appear at once. Walking up and down the terrace at Rambouillet...considering the causes of the impotence which had deprived us in the past—that is, the bankruptcy of governmental power—I resolved more firmly not to let my own be infringed. The mission with which I was invested seemed as clear as it could be. Getting into the car to drive to Paris, I felt myself simultaneously gripped by emotion and filled with serenity."[4]

In the execution of his design, de Gaulle proceeded first to the war ministry, the perceived seat of power in the capital, and then to the police station, where he knew control over the local gendarmerie could be maintained. He shunned a group of local resistance leaders who were waiting for him at the Hotel de Ville, insisting that they should come to him. Representatives of the provisional government and the resistance had met previously, and now it was time for the leader to assert his authority. However, the process must be carefully managed, sending a clear message in its execution.

It was early evening when he finally reached the Hotel de Ville, where he met these fighters, Gaullist and communist, nationalist and anti-Nazi, who had struggled four long years and known this leader only through photographs and as a voice over the radio. De Gaulle delivered no flowery speech and offered no words of gratitude. Instead, his brief comments went to the heart of the business at hand. He stated clearly that the will of the people was for a Republican form of government. It would follow that the resistance would adhere to that government, its useful purpose having been fulfilled with the defeat of the Germans. Well after 8 p.m., de Gaulle finally showed himself to the people of Paris, leaning from a small balcony above the square outside the hotel, where thousands had gathered and waited for several hours.

A grand parade was scheduled for the following day, and Leclerc's division was to participate in the demonstration of stability under de Gaulle's leadership. However, Leclerc and the 2nd Armored were still under the direct battlefield command of American General Leonard Gerow, commander of the Allied V Army Corps. Gerow needed troops to continue the eastward push beyond Paris and ordered Leclerc to rejoin the general advance. However, when de Gaulle learned of the situation, his response was characteristic. He appeared surprised at Gerow's lack of understanding and informed the general that Leclerc would be taking orders from the leader of his government. French troops were to be commanded ultimately by the French head of state.

As more than a million people crowded the route, Charles de Gaulle walked along the Champs Élysées to the Place de la Concorde, a covey of resistance leaders well behind him. During the moment, even the placement in the procession of those who had fought for the liberation was choreographed to assert his authority. Even as he walked, that authority was being exercised across France as Gaullist representatives took control in provincial capitals and smaller cities and towns, quelling any potential bid for power, particularly by communist elements in the south. Pragmatic as necessary, de Gaulle did appoint a select few communists to positions within the government.

In his memoirs, de Gaulle recalled the emotion of the triumphal parade.

> Ah! It was the sea! An enormous crowd packed tight on either side of the roadway. As far as I could see it was nothing but one living

swell in the sunlight and under the tricolor. Since everyone there had in his heart chosen Charles de Gaulle as refuge from his suffering and symbol of his hope, it was important that he should see him, familiar and fraternal, and that at this sight the nation's unity should blaze out. It is true that I have neither the appearance or the liking for attitudes and gestures that can please an audience. But I am sure they did not expect them.

So, I walked on, quiet and deeply moved in the midst of the crowd's indescribable exultation, through a storm of voices that echoed my name. At that moment there was occurring one of those miracles of national consciousness, one of those gestures on the part of France that in the course of centuries sometimes come to light in our history. And I, in the middle of this passionate outburst, I felt that I was fulfilling a function that went far, far beyond myself personally, that of acting as the instrument of destiny.[5]

From the Place de la Concorde, de Gaulle took a car to the Cathedral of Notre Dame to attend a brief service of thanksgiving. As he stepped from the car, two young girls came forward and offered flowers. At that moment, shots rang out in the crowded street. Spectators ran for cover, and firing back in the direction of the first shot was indiscriminate. Unruffled but momentarily trapped against the cathedral door by the pressing crowd, de Gaulle finally collected himself and proceeded inside. Then, a rifle crackled a second time, apparently from high above the choir loft. Undeterred, the general continued down the aisle to his seat, a distance of nearly 200 feet.

Those who witnessed the display of literal coolness under fire were amazed. A BBC reporter confessed, "He walked straight ahead in what appeared to me to be a hail of fire, without hesitation, his shoulders flung back. It was the most extraordinary display of courage that I've ever seen." Another reporter commented that the performance ensured that de Gaulle had France in the palm of his hand.

Whether these incidents were random acts of violence or assassination attempts has never been determined. However, just the evening before two armed men had been arrested at the Hotel de Ville. One of them had been a Vichy agent, and their intent to kill de Gaulle was clear. But de Gaulle shrugged at the shooting at Notre Dame and termed it a vulgar piece of showing off.

In reconstituting the French government, de Gaulle had refused to acknowledge the legitimacy of what had taken place at Vichy. He further realized that the Third Republic had met its demise in 1940. Therefore, he asserted that his claim to authority had come directly from the people—the ultimate authority. In October 1944, Albert Lebrun, former president of the Third Republic who had never officially resigned, called on de Gaulle and expressed his support for the new government. The debate between Washington, DC, and London as to how to deal with de Gaulle entered a new phase. There was little lingering doubt as to how much power he held in France.

Both the United States and Britain solidified their diplomatic ties in Paris, but Roosevelt stubbornly refused to offer de Gaulle full recognition. Churchill remained loyal, however, though he was still miffed at the French leader for refusing to see him in Algiers in August prior to the relocation of the government to Paris. Roosevelt dispatched an ambassador to France, Jefferson Caffrey, but the US government still did not officially recognize France. For de Gaulle, it was all or nothing. Therefore, he refused to meet Caffrey and treated the British ambassador, Duff Cooper, in the same manner.

Clearly, de Gaulle had the support of Eisenhower, whose hands were full with military matters and wished to be absolved of the responsibility for any civil administration in France as soon as possible. Churchill was under increasing pressure from the media and members of Parliament in London to insist that the Americans recognize de Gaulle's government, and it was readily apparent to most observers that de Gaulle was firmly in control of the liberated areas of France in the autumn of 1944. Still, Roosevelt refused to recognize the de Gaulle government until a well-defined "zone of the interior" that was free of combat could be identified within France.

At long last, on October 20, Eisenhower informed the White House that such a zone had been identified. Grudgingly, with his last objection overcome and in the midst of his campaign for an unprecedented fourth term as president of the United States, Roosevelt relented. On October 23, 1944, the United States, Great Britain, and the Soviet Union each issued a communiqué of full diplomatic recognition for the government of France.

Two days later, de Gaulle issued a simple statement. "The French government is satisfied to be called by its name."[6]

When British ambassador Duff Cooper commented at dinner on October 23 that he was certain de Gaulle was relieved that the affair was over, the French leader replied that it never really would be over. De Gaulle would never forget that Churchill and Britain had sided with Roosevelt time after time during the crucial war years rather than with another traditionally powerful European state—France. This long-standing resentment reared its ugly head years later with his veto of British entry into the European Common Market.

At the same time de Gaulle insisted that French forces remain with the Allied armies advancing into Germany, he also wrangled with Stalin over questions of Polish sovereignty, the influence of the French communist party, and other issues during a visit to Moscow in the winter of 1944. Questions remained concerning the future of the French colonies in North Africa, the Middle East, and Indochina. British intervention in Syria was eerily reminiscent of the Fashoda Incident, which de Gaulle had never forgotten. He flew into a rage when it appeared that France was once again being forced to acquiesce to a superior British military presence. The business of government would be an awesome future burden.

During the final months of World War II, while he dealt with the practical problems of food and shelter for the French people and pacifying radical elements of the former resistance, de Gaulle moved as swiftly as possible to exercise justice against the Vichy collaborationists. Although it was imperative that high-ranking members of the Vichy government should be tried, there were also summary executions and murders, and old scores were settled without sanction by the government. Officially, fewer than 800 individuals were tried and executed for collaboration between June 1944 and May 1945; however, many thousands were executed out of hand. The trials of Vichy collaborators were not completed until 1949.

The two most prominent Vichyites, Pétain and Laval, had been taken into custody by the Germans in August 1944 and held in an old Hohenzollern castle on the edge of the Black Forest. At his own request, Pétain was released by the Germans and transported to Switzerland. Although de Gaulle would have preferred that he live out his days in exile in the neighboring country, Pétain believed the only honorable course of action was to return to France. On April 26, 1945, he was driven to the French border, placed under arrest, and then transported by train to Paris and prison at Fort Montrouge. Laval was imprisoned there as well.

On July 23, the trial of Pétain got under way. During three weeks of testimony, Pétain spoke only once. The outcome of the proceedings was never really in doubt, and on August 15 he was found guilty of treason by a unanimous vote of the Paris tribunal. He was later sentenced to death by a vote of 14 to 13; however, it was the desire of both the court and de Gaulle that the sentence be commuted to life in prison. This was accomplished, and the 89-year-old marshal was banished to prison on the windswept Ile d'Yeu off the Atlantic coast of France, where he died in 1951. The odious Laval was sentenced to death in October and executed by firing squad. De Gaulle was virtually silent with regard to Pétain during the proceedings against the marshal and in the years that followed.

When Roosevelt, Churchill, and Stalin met at the Black Sea resort town of Yalta in the Crimea during January 1945, the French government was excluded. De Gaulle was dismayed but not surprised and took to the radio to state that France would not be bound by any decisions made to which its government had not been a party. As it turned out, the conference ended with favorable results. France was given a zone of occupation both in Germany and in Berlin, appointed a member of the council that would govern postwar Germany, asked to endorse the conference that would draft the charter of the United Nations, and guaranteed a permanent seat on the proposed UN security council. Needless to say, these favorable measures were accomplished with much debate. Within three months, Roosevelt was dead, and Harry S. Truman was the new US president.

When World War II in Europe came to an end on May 8, 1945, relations between France and her wartime Allies were in many ways worse than they had been for some time. Truman threatened to suspend aid to France in response to de Gaulle's intransigence on troop dispositions in Germany. Churchill was railing against de Gaulle over political and military concerns in the Middle East. When the prime minister met with Stalin and Truman at Potsdam on the outskirts of Berlin in mid-July, de Gaulle was again excluded. However, France was formally invited to join in the council of major powers that would meet for a number of years to come in order to discuss issues of worldwide importance. Of more immediate impact, Churchill was voted out of office and Clement Attlee of the opposition Labour Party became prime minister of Great Britain.

By the autumn of 1945, Charles de Gaulle could feel the wind of change in his own land. On October 21, a referendum had confirmed the wishes of the people that an assembly be convened to create a new constitution. The assembly was to be of seven months' duration, and its elected membership consisted of communists, socialists, and political moderates. The communists had gained the most seats, but none of the factions carried a clear majority, and coalition government appeared a foregone conclusion. On November 13, de Gaulle was elected president of France; however, his power was substantially curtailed. He could not intervene in the affairs of the assembly, which had been duly elected—and he was not even a member.

By December, the handwriting was on the wall. The majority of those in the assembly were in favor of a constitution that resembled that of the Third Republic, one in which the legislative body was foremost and the president had little ability to influence and could not dissolve. De Gaulle considered such a government a failure and believed this conviction had been validated by the calamity of 1940. He favored a strong presidency, such as exhibited by his personal leadership of the provisional government from Algiers to Paris during the latter years of the war. He paused to reflect and made the decision to resign from the government. Perhaps it was a fitting end to a turbulent era.

On January 14, 1946, he called the various ministers of government to a meeting in his office at the war ministry. As they all stood, he told them in a statement that had been carefully crafted, "The exclusive regime of the political parties has returned. I condemn it. However, unless I use force to impose a dictatorship, which I do not desire and which would doubtless come to a bad end, I have no means of preventing this experiment. So I must retire."

In a matter of minutes, it was over. Charles de Gaulle had become a private citizen. As he left his office, his mind may well have wandered back to a comment during a dinner meeting two years earlier. When a young member of his staff had asked about his plans for the future, de Gaulle responded, "As for me, I shall withdraw. . . . I have a mission, and it is coming to an end. I must disappear. France may again one day have need of a pure image. That image must be left with her. Had Joan of Arc been married, she would no longer have been Joan of Arc. I must disappear."[7]

CHAPTER 8

Vive la France

PERHAPS THE GREATEST MISCALCULATION OF CHARLES DE GAULLE'S political life was his belief that the people of France would rise in unison to sweep him back into office from a brief retirement. He had never been a rich man, and while he brooded in a small apartment residence furnished by the government he wondered why the crowds had not come. While he was certainly an astute politician and the idea that the French people would clamor for his immediate return may have too much for even the grand de Gaulle to deem realistic, he asked an aide to venture down the street and see if indeed the police had erected barricades or checkpoints to keep the people away.

France, still in the throes of economic chaos and political division, seemed to have no time to remember the strong-hearted leader who had emerged to save the honor of the country, even though the nation's hour of deliverance from the Nazis had been only months in the past. Meanwhile, the creation of a new constitutional government, which de Gaulle thought was doomed to fail, moved ponderously forward. Communist vied with socialist, fascist, and moderate to form a government and craft a constitution acceptable to the people. Finally, the Fourth Republic came into being in the autumn of 1946.

On the second anniversary of his historic return to French soil, June 16, 1946, de Gaulle journeyed to Bayeaux, where he had greeted a frenzied crowd on that blustery day in 1944. Months of stony silence were broken.

> It is from the head of state, placed above the parties, elected by a college including the assembly, but much wider and made up in such a way as to make him the president of the French union as well as of the republic, that the executive power must proceed. It is the task of the head of State to reconcile the general interest, where appointments are concerned, with the direction that emerges from the assembly. It will be his job to appoint ministers and, first of all, of course, the prime minister. It is the job of the head of State to promulgate laws and issue decrees. He presides over the Councils of the Government. He serves as an arbiter above political contingencies. It is his duty, if the nation is in danger, to guarantee national independence.[1]

The Bayeaux speech embodied the mind-set of Charles de Gaulle and marked his reentry into the discourse of French politics. His vision of government would save France from the calamity of factional infighting and the heavy hand of a dictatorship. His presidency would provide the leadership and fortitude to appoint ministers of worth, maintain a foremost position for France among nations, and dissolve the assembly and call for new elections if necessary.

To some, the speech smacked of a strange right-wing perspective, but such was not his intent. He had always been the master manipulator, playing East against West, pitting ally against ally. De Gaulle was certain that upon his triumphant return to power, he would again place France cleverly between the United States and Great Britain to the west and the Soviet Union to the east, favoring a pan-European consensus. Until that time, he must rise above the petty partisan politics of the assembly, remaining somewhat aloof but always ready to rise—pure and without stain—a modern Joan of Arc.

The only real estate that Charles de Gaulle ever owned was his family home at Colombey-les-Deux-Églises, which had been damaged during the war. Following lengthy repairs, it was suitable in the spring of 1946 for the family, Charles, Yvonne, and Anne, to return for the first time since 1939. Their son, Philippe, had married and continued a career in the navy. A grandson, fittingly named Charles de Gaulle, was born. Their daughter Elizabeth had also married, and her husband, a young army officer, would serve his father-in-law in later years as an aide.

On February 6, 1948, Anne, the daughter born with Down syndrome and to whom he had shown the most human tenderness of his adult life, died of pneumonia just days after her twentieth birthday. As the grief-stricken parents walked away from the grave in the small cemetery at Colombey-les-deux-Églises, Charles murmured to his wife, "Maintenant, elle est comme les autres," or "Now, she is like all the rest."[2]

He had been a heavy smoker his entire life, and during that same year he quit the habit at the age of 58. Doctors had advised that he stop, fearing it was contributing to worsening eyesight. Although he missed the cigarette or cigar greatly and bemoaned the loss of a pleasure, he had announced his intent to others. Therefore, since he had committed rather publicly the decision could not be reversed. In 1952, he underwent cataract surgery.

As private citizens, the family experienced some rather lean times. A Douglas DC-4 Skymaster aircraft that had been given to Charles by President Harry Truman was turned over to the French air force. The luxury Cadillac presented to him by President Eisenhower as a gift was surrendered as well, and a small French car was purchased. Yvonne learned to drive.

The pension of a brigadier was rather paltry; however, when an initiative to raise his rank to that of full general or possibly even to Marshal of France was put forth he summarily brushed it off. The additional money would be welcome, but not at the price of personal dignity. He remarked that no one had seen fit to suggest such a promotion during the dark days of World War II and that to do so at such a late date was utterly ridiculous.[3]

Some de Gaulle biographers have described the years that followed World War II as the "wandering in the desert," a time during which the man of destiny believed that his mission was incomplete. Certainly, he had saved the nation's honor and led the restoration of its self-government; however, it was a form of government with which he was at odds, and above all the international prestige and true greatness of France had yet to be restored. Somehow, he knew that the day of opportunity, the day when he would be called upon once more, would come. The days in between, though, were long indeed.

In the winter of 1947, de Gaulle made perhaps the greatest political faux pas of his lifetime. He consulted with old associates and determined that in order to hasten his return to power an entry into the political arena was indeed necessary. Although he disdained the political parties, there might be an avenue of approach that could accomplish what was necessary. To answer this need, de Gaulle and his associates created the Rally of the French People (*Rassemblement du Peuple Français,* or RPF). The RPF was to be, in essence, a voice of opposition. It was not to be a political party but would function as the foil of the government, appealing directly to the people for their votes and support.

At the cliffs of Bruneval on March 30, 1947, he proclaimed to a large crowd, "The day will come when, rejecting the sterile games, and reforming the poorly constructed framework in which the nation is losing its way and the state disqualifying itself, the great mass of the French people will rally around France!"[4]

With nearly a million applications for membership within the first month of its existence, the RPF gained momentum quickly and its candidates garnered 40 percent of the vote during the municipal elections held across France in October 1947 as the French people sought stability and leadership in their government.

The Fourth Republic fended off a challenge to its authority and skirted a movement to hold a national election that might have catapulted the RPF and its standoffish leader into power. There were incidents of violence between de Gaulle's RPF bodyguards and communist agitators. The most serious of these occurred following a rally in Grenoble in September 1948, when one communist was killed and more than a dozen people were wounded. An official investigation ensued and some of de Gaulle's followers were charged with responding to sticks and stones with bullets.

In the early 1950s, as economic conditions improved throughout Europe largely because of massive Marshall Plan aid from the United States and the Cold War began to settle in, an uneasy status quo developed between East and West, and the RPF began to lose momentum almost as quickly as it had begun. By the summer of 1951, the RPF held only 120 seats in the assembly, far from a controlling majority, but de Gaulle was adamant. There would be no coalition government if he were to lead. The RPF would remain in opposition.

Predictably, there were RPF men who felt it their patriotic duty to work with the government, particularly during difficult times that included growing issues with France's colonial empire in Indochina and economic instability which spiraled out of control and precipitated a run on the franc. By the summer of 1952, one of de Gaulle's associates had been approached about forming a coalition government, and as the year waned approximately 25 percent of the RPF faithful had broken ranks. Eventually, de Gaulle publicly announced that these former RPF members were not acting in the name of the organization or, more important, in his own name.

Nearly six years after the formation of the RPF, which had begun with a great deal of promise, it ended in disappointment. Standing in opposition was familiar territory to the former leader; however, attempting to return to power through popular election was a process with which he had virtually no experience and for which he harbored more contempt than ardor. Born in response to the creation of the Fourth Republic, the RPF maintained the focus of the French people on the failings of the fragile government. At the same time, the Truman Doctrine, the assertion of the US president that his country would vehemently oppose the spread of communism, escalated the Cold War and brought France precariously closer to the Western orbit.

De Gaulle concluded that a return to power would not be accomplished through the electoral process. His original premise had been correct all along. Some great event would take place, and he would be called upon to lead once again. When that time came, an organization in place within the government would be useful. He had not realized the value of such a structure earlier in his political career, but now maintained relations with individuals he referred to as "friends in the assembly."

When de Gaulle formally announced in July 1955 that he would once again withdraw from political life, he had been compelled to acknowledge that the RPF had been a strategic failure. For its leader, however, it provided a deeper understanding of France, its people, and its place in the modern world. He had engaged the average Frenchman in dialogue and gained insight into the nature of political compromise. The experience would serve him well in the future.

During the course of his life, Charles de Gaulle was a prolific author and writer. Over the course of more than 60 years, he authored 13 published books, 35,000 letters, and five volumes of speeches. He was precise with punctuation and wrote always in flowing longhand with black ink. In 1952, as the RPF was unwinding, he began his most significant literary undertaking, *War Memoirs*. His withdrawal and subsequent time away from the public eye allowed him to reflect in a manner that had not been his privilege previously. The pages were typed by his daughter Elizabeth, and within five weeks of publication in October 1954 more than 100,000 copies of the first volume, *The Appeal*, were sold.

The work is artistic, moving, and eloquent. Author Charles Williams commented, "The *Memoires de Guerre* are without doubt a major work of French literature in their own right. The language is noble, the analysis profound and the sweep heroic. Of course, it would be missing the point to take the General's account of his life up to that date as an attempt at unbiased and objective history. They are more to be regarded as a personal apologia for his own role in the great dramas through which he had lived. As such, it need hardly be said, they frequently seem to view events through a badly distorted lens."[5]

The *War Memoirs* reflect the de Gaulle perspective, the resolute, defiant de Gaulle shaped by a sense of destiny, hardened by war and political adversity, yet tempered by the personal cost of a long road already traveled and tinged with a glimpse of human emotion rarely seen in the stoic facade of a general. He was an author virtually to his dying day, and the income from his literary work provided seed money for a foundation in memory of the dear departed Anne.

As de Gaulle labored to complete *War Memoirs* and come to terms with the apparent failure of the RPF, world events were swirling around him. It is quite doubtful that he would have acquiesced to the formality of an integrated command structure for NATO, although he did welcome the military alliance that was born in 1949, since it more fully defined the commitment of the United States to the security of Western Europe. No doubt, he would have opposed the rearming of France's traditional enemy, a now divided Germany. He did decry the formation of the European Coal and Steel Community, which had been proposed by the government of the Fourth Republic in the spring of 1950 and later formed a basis for the European Common Market and included concessions on the control of France's industrial base.

Meanwhile, France was losing its grip on Indochina. The disastrous defeat at Dien Bien Phu occurred in the spring of 1954, and within a month a new prime minister, Pierre Mendes-France, took office. A wartime associate of de Gaulle, Mendes-France moved to extricate France from the losing proposition in Indochina and negotiated an agreement that granted independence to Laos, Cambodia, and a divided Vietnam, where elections were to be held. In Africa, discussions were undertaken to provide a path toward independence for Tunisia.

Algeria, however, was a different story. Although a governor general exercised authority there, it was actually considered by most Frenchmen to be a part of the French republic rather than a colony. Violence between separatists and those intent on retaining Algeria within the French fold had erupted in the autumn of 1954, and no expedient solution could be determined. The French army, acquainted with defeat during the previous two decades, would not go quietly this time, and the realization of this weighed heavily on the Fourth Republic. The Algerian Front de Libération Nationale (FLN) was just as intent on separation.

De Gaulle had always refused to be boxed in on the question of independence for portions of France's colonial empire, and in the summer of 1955 he commented that an "association" with the North African states might serve as a more acceptable framework for the future. His choice of the word "association" was deliberately vague. He remained quiet and aloof, and those who sought his opinions on world events often emerged with contradictory perspectives on the general's positions. He did go so far as to issue a statement that he did not endorse any reports attributed to comments he made on any topic which were reported to have taken place in private.

Vagueness on the Algerian question was an important part of de Gaulle's grand design. His own return to power might be facilitated as long as the issue remained unresolved, symptomatic of an indecisive government that could not control the course of events. The absence of a commitment one way or the other would leave him free to act. The strategy was pragmatic politics and vintage de Gaulle. Meanwhile, the Gaullists both within and outside the government were working to hasten the day of their leader's return.

In the spring of 1958, the prospect of civil war in France was very real. Elements within the army had conspired to take control of the government, and one of the numerous unsteady governments of the Fourth Republic collapsed in April. A phone call to de Gaulle from representatives of the Fourth Republic to ask under what conditions he might entertain forming a government was rebuffed as premature. Within days, an angry mob stormed the offices of the governor general in Algiers. The army leadership vowed that it would not stand for the formation of any government that might open negotiations with the FLN.

Walking a political tightrope, de Gaulle waited while the nation clamored to hear his voice. The army might seize control of the government in Paris as he remained silent; however, moving too quickly would place him in the same precarious position as the teetering final government of the Fourth Republic, which had been hastily installed by a vote of the near panicked assembly.

Finally, at 5 p.m. on the afternoon of May 15, 1958, de Gaulle concluded that the moment had come. He released a statement that read in part, "Once before, from the depths of the abyss, the nation placed its confidence in me to lead it back to salvation. Today, with the new trials crowding in on it, it is right that it should know that I am ready to assume the powers of the republic."[6]

As the situation continued to deteriorate, paratroopers of the French army based in Algeria seized control of the island of Corsica in a bloodless assault, and the local police force joined in. News subsequently reached de Gaulle that the military jump-off from Corsica to the mainland of France would occur within hours. A few words from the old general put the uprising in check. Even so, detractors railed that de Gaulle was intent on becoming a dictator, taking advantage of the political turmoil to exert power with which he had not been vested.

Two weeks after his statement to the French people, de Gaulle presented his conditions for the formation of a government. He would exercise full power during a limited emergency period with the assembly in recess, while the new government would be authorized to draw up a new constitution, which would be put to popular vote. In December 1958, de Gaulle was elected President of the Fifth Republic, leading a government that closely resembled his vision at Bayeux in June 1946.

Quickly, the new government was approved, and cabinet positions were filled. Three days later, de Gaulle was on the ground in Algiers and received a tumultuous welcome. He immediately exerted the force of personality necessary to bring chaos into some semblance of order. The mere presence of de Gaulle was a calming influence, and he expressed a willingness to resolve the issue of Algerian independence while suppressing those who opposed discussions with the separatists.

However, the road to independence for Algeria remained long, and negotiations with leaders of the FLN were not undertaken until the summer of 1960. The question of Algerian self-determination was put to the people. In France, 76 percent of the vote favored Algeria charting its own course. In Algeria, the vote was 70 percent in favor. After nearly a year of further negotiations, Algeria became an independent nation on July 3, 1962. The Algerian exercise had not been without personal hazard. At least nine attempts on de Gaulle's life had been made by extremists both in favor of Algerian independence and opposed to it, and a couple of these nearly succeeded.

The rise of Charles de Gaulle in 1958 was a watershed moment in the history of France. Through tremendous force of character, a single-minded will, and exceptional leadership de Gaulle brought France back from the precipice of chaos and national upheaval. Perhaps the greatest service he rendered to the nation after World War II was extricating it from the long, costly war in Algeria, which could never be won militarily and was settled with honor through a process toward peace.

For 11 more years, Charles de Gaulle served as French head of state. His foreign policy pursued a hard line based on what he believed to be French interests. Foremost here was a continuing paranoia regarding the intent of the United States and Great Britain to relegate France to the status of a second-tier power, and de Gaulle took advantage of every opportunity to assert a "continental" policy for Europe, which he proclaimed should be free from the Atlantic to the Urals of heavy-handed outside influence.

The French government under de Gaulle identified a series of major objectives. Among these were the complete independence of France in political, military, and defense decision making and policy, a nuclear-capable French armed forces, which would give the nation standing among the world's great powers, and the end of full French participation in NATO and of the organization's command structure in Europe while the 20-year American commitment to the security of Western Europe continued as specified in the NATO treaty of 1949.

Further, the government of the Fifth Republic sought to establish France as the leader of a cooperative political, military, and economic system under the auspices of the European Common Market. France would hold veto power on matters of policy while excluding Great Britain from the Common Market as long as that nation retained such close ties to the United States that the welfare of continental Europe was considered secondary by British leaders.

De Gaulle's stated goal for the Common Market was "to make this European organization one of three world powers and, if need be one day, the arbiter between the two camps, the Soviet and the Anglo-Saxon."[7]

In his effort to promote the sovereignty of France as a European power, de Gaulle refused to accept the offer of US nuclear missiles without the freedom of independent action on their use. De Gaulle likewise would not allow the placement of nuclear weapons under US control in France. Instead, France conducted its own successful nuclear bomb test in the Algerian desert in 1960, and a program of nuclear armament followed.

De Gaulle also reasoned that neither France nor greater Europe would fight in any conflict unless it controlled its own military. Therefore, France must be outside the NATO alliance and thus outside the umbrella of American hegemony. Although France continued to cooperate with the West under the original Atlantic Treaty, de Gaulle took his country out of the military alliance on March 7, 1966.

Fearing that Britain was no more than a Trojan Horse for US interference in Europe, and citing the fundamental differences between the British economy and that of the continental nations, including ties to the global Commonwealth and a relatively minor agricultural market sector, de Gaulle vetoed British entry into the European Common Market on January 14, 1963. It was not until a decade later, three years after de Gaulle's death, that the island nation gained entry.

Seeking closer ties with the Federal Republic of Germany, de Gaulle signed a treaty of cooperation with Chancellor Konrad Adenauer a week after his veto of British entry into the Common Market. His hope was that stronger ties would solidify Western Europe as a force in world politics and perhaps enhance the leadership role of France on the European continent. Although the two leaders forged a new era of cooperation, de Gaulle was disappointed that Adenauer remained a staunch supporter of NATO.

During the mid-1960s, the French president stepped further into the global political arena. To the great consternation of the United

States, France recognized the People's Republic of China in 1964. De Gaulle railed against US military involvement in Vietnam and opened a period of détente with the Soviet Union scarcely four years after assuring the US government during the Cuban Missile Crisis that France would stand with the Kennedy administration in the event of war.

A historic visit to Canada in the summer of 1967 was cut short following de Gaulle's exhortation of "Vive le Québec Libre!" or "Long live free Quebec!" an obvious reference to the separatist movement in the French-speaking province and an embarrassment to the Canadian government.

He reached out to the nations of the emerging Third World, offering French economic aid and his own leadership. In this context, the former French empire provided a political bridgehead to underdeveloped nations.[8]

While debate continues as to the effectiveness of de Gaulle's foreign policy, he was successful in raising his country to prominence. Due to his antagonism and mistrust of a perceived Anglo-American conspiracy against France, he maintained the military alliance outside the NATO command structure. He saw US détente emerge with the Soviet Union and the People's Republic of China, which diminished the role of France as a potential political arbiter. He also found that France could not assert the leadership role he envisioned in Western Europe due to the burgeoning strength of the German economy and that nation's refusal to distance itself from the United States. Although his rationale was understood, the veto of British entry into the Common Market smacked of vindictiveness.

On the domestic front, Charles de Gaulle always believed that he derived power from the consent of the people. Therefore, despite his own virtual domination of the French government, he essentially circumvented his own constitution, bypassing the assembly in the summer of 1962 and putting a referendum before the public to allow the popular election of future presidents of France rather than election by vote of the assembly as had been the practice for 150 years. The assembly objected loudly, and the president responded by dissolving the body and calling for new elections. In the meantime, 62 percent of the vote favored the change in the presidential election process, validating de Gaulle's political strength.

The text of the constitution was open to interpretation, and in each case when a question emerged de Gaulle acted on the premise that the authority of the president was supreme. However, the assembly was the legislative body of government and de Gaulle needed to maintain either an outright Gaullist majority or working majority in cooperation with centrist elements. This was a continual thorn in his side, as de Gaulle had long wished to be a head of government who was not tied to the principles or political sway of a particular party.

From 1962 to 1968, the government of Charles de Gaulle may be likened in many ways to that of a benevolent dictator—always believing that he derived authority from the people, surrounding himself with cabinet ministers who essentially performed his bidding, and manipulating the office of the prime minister as he saw fit. According to him, the president was charged with governing based on the authority of the state, while the prime minister was vested with the duty of conducting the day-to-day affairs of government.

Often enough, de Gaulle became involved in those daily affairs as well. He frequently announced policies or courses of action without consulting his ministers. As his days lengthened, he expanded the scope of presidential authority, justifying these actions on the basis of a broad interpretation of the constitution. Adding to his prestige was the lengthy period of economic expansion enjoyed not only by France but all of Western Europe from 1958 to 1967.

Ironically, the foundation for this economic recovery following World War II and the ensuing years of growth was the result of the work of the much maligned Fourth Republic, which judiciously invested Marshall Plan funds and entered into the agreement that formed the European Coal and Steel Community, the basis for the

Common Market. Had de Gaulle returned to power prior to 1958, it is quite likely that French policy would have proved an impediment to a broad recovery.

Nonetheless, there was something unsettled in the spirit of France, and even in the midst of a resurgent prosperity the people were never wholly satisfied with their improving standard of living. According to several polls during the 1960s, satisfaction with economic policy remained regularly below 50 percent although the overall popularity of the venerable president never dipped below that threshold.

When de Gaulle stood for reelection in 1965, it was with the expectation that the direct vote of the people would extend his mandate. After all, it was he who had brought an end to the election of the president through a grand council of local and national politicians. The will of the people would be expressed at the polls.

In something of a shock, the French restlessness made itself heard when de Gaulle received less than 44 percent of the vote, while his rivals François Mitterand and Jean Lecanuet received just over 32 and nearly 16 percent respectively. The resulting runoff, which de Gaulle won with 54.4 percent to Mitterand's 45.5 was a hollow victory. The process had been a blow to both presidential and personal prestige. Following the parliamentary elections held two years later, the Gaullists were compelled to form a coalition government and maintained their simple majority by only a single seat.

By the spring of 1968, France had slipped into the doldrums of day-to-day existence, and de Gaulle's economic policy, which included an insistence on a balanced budget and a high relative value of the franc, had curbed expansion and resulted in rising unemployment. The autocratic de Gaulle had governed for nearly a decade, and beneath the surface lay a growing discontent. In May, students demonstrated in part due to the lack of access to an educational system that could not accommodate a growing population. In the same month, disruptive labor strikes threatened to topple the de Gaulle government. A common thread of dissatisfaction with authoritative rule ran through the crowded streets of France's major cities.

Caught up in changing times, it was difficult for the aging president to grasp the individualism and freedom of expression that were sweeping the globe during that turbulent year. The upheaval was the very antithesis of order, allegiance to a strong state, and a notion of grandeur. This was chaos.

Early in the crisis, de Gaulle refused to take the demonstrators seriously. He contemplated sending troops to restore order but in the end refrained from pitting countrymen against one another in what would have been a clear escalation of the violence. For the first time in his political life, the president wavered and seemed uncertain of the proper course of action. Perhaps it was age or fatigue. More likely it was the difficulty in clearly identifying the nature and vigor of the opposition.

While de Gaulle seemed detached and perplexed, Prime Minister Georges Pompidou led a government effort to negotiate with the unions and identify specifics that could be discussed and negotiated. Meanwhile, the political opposition seized the moment, particularly the left with Mitterand stepping forward as the potential leader of a new government.

At this hour of peril, the de Gaulle flair for the dramatic emerged once again. On the morning of May 29, he abruptly canceled a cabinet meeting. A short while later, he told an aide that he was tired and wanted to rest at his home in Colombey-le-deux-Églises. His ministers were alarmed and unaware that he had departed. Soon it became clear that, in fact, he had simply disappeared. Rumors began to swirl around the capital city. Had the president abdicated? Was he incapacitated? Had the stout resolution of his character failed him at last?

Rather than flying directly to his home, the president and his wife headed eastward to the German city of Baden-Baden, where French forces were stationed in the Black Forest. For approximately 90 minutes the president of France was engaged in discussions with General Jacques Massu, the commander of French troops in Germany. Massu had supported de Gaulle's return to power in 1958 and apparently retained the president's confidence, although their contact had been limited in recent years.

The exact nature of the meeting remains shrouded in mystery. Truly, no one knows whether de Gaulle had contemplated leaving office or had simply slipped away to gather himself for the high theater that was to come within hours. In the early evening of May 29, he arrived at Colombey-les-deux-Églises, picked up the telephone, and notified Secretary General Bernard Tricot that he would return to Paris the following day and address the nation on the radio.

At 4:30 p.m. on May 30, de Gaulle took to the airwaves, renewed and vigorous. "Being the custodian of national and republican sovereignty," he stated forcefully, "I have envisaged for the past 24 hours all eventualities, without exception, that might allow me to maintain it. I have made my decisions. In the present circumstances, I will not retire. I have a mandate from the people. I will fulfill it. I will not change the prime minister, whose courage, solidity and capacity merit the homage of all.... Today, I am dissolving the national assembly."[9]

Accounts of the events of May 29–30, including those of Massu and Pompidou, indicate a personal crisis in confidence for de Gaulle. On the other hand, all the years of personal strength, resolution, and purpose could not desert him in the twilight of his public life. As great leaders must do—and as he had done countless times in the past—Charles de Gaulle reached deeply within himself and found the fortitude to carry on. Among the more immediate events that undoubtedly buttressed his will were the announcement of Mitterand and the rise of the communist political voice. These presented clear challenges to the authority of the government, adversaries that de Gaulle could identify, confront, and subdue.

Following the radio address, a massive demonstration in favor of the government took place in Paris. The crisis ebbed. Considering these events, which occurred in rapid succession, one of two extremes must be acknowledged. Either de Gaulle had neared the precipice of failure and somehow pulled back, or the masterful leader had deliberately extricated himself momentarily from the maelstrom and returned with precise timing to restore order as only he was able. The former is quite human, the latter sublime. In either case, it was a masterstroke.

The elections that followed the turbulent spring of 1968 resulted in a decisive landslide for the Gaullists. However, their leader knew that his desire for certain reforms in education and other areas of importance would be met with resistance from the conservative politicians of his own party, elected on the basis of a return to order. De Gaulle scheduled a referendum on several rather minor points in early 1969, and soon afterward it became apparent that the measures would be defeated. Originally, the referendum had been intended as an affirmation of the president's bond with his people. Instead, it served as a means of exiting office with grace and prestige intact. Pompidou, who had risen to the occasion during the crisis of the previous year, was waiting in the wings.

Within 15 minutes of the polls closing on April 25, it was clear that the referendum would be defeated. In short order came the announcement. "I cease to exercise my functions as president of the republic. This decision is effective at noon today."[10]

Following his retirement, de Gaulle visited Ireland and Spain and settled at Colombey-les-deux-Églises to craft *Memoirs of Hope*. On the morning of November 9, 1970, only 13 days before his eightieth birthday, he rose and set to work on the third chapter of *Endeavor*, the second volume of *Memoirs of Hope*. He wrote some brief correspondence and chatted with a neighbor. Prior to the evening news broadcast, he sat down to a game of solitaire. Moments later he was unconscious, and within the hour the greatest Frenchman of modern times was dead of a ruptured abdominal aorta.

Years earlier, he had dictated the terms of his final farewell. The directions were given in straightforward de Gaulle fashion.

"I desire my funeral to take place at Colombey-les-deux-Églises," he wrote on January 16, 1952.

If I die elsewhere my body must be taken home without any public ceremony whatever.

My grave will be the one in which my daughter Anne lies and where one day my wife also will lie. Inscription: "Charles de Gaulle, 1890–..." Nothing more.

The ceremony will be arranged by my son, my daughter, my son-in-law, my daughter-in-law, assisted by my private office, in such a way that it is extremely simple. I want no national funeral. No president, no minister, no representatives from the assembly or any other corporate body. Only the French Army may participate officially, as such, but their participation must be on a very modest scale, without music, fanfare or ringing of bells.

No speech must be delivered, either in the church or elsewhere. No funeral oration in the assembly. No seats must be reserved during the ceremony except for my family, my close friends, members of the Order of the Liberation, and the municipal council of Colombey.

Men and women of France and of other countries may, if they so wish, pay my memory the homage of accompanying my body to its last resting place. But it is my wish that this should be carried out in silence.

I wish to refuse in advance any distinction, promotion, dignity, citation, decoration, whether French or foreign. And if any is accorded me, it will be in violation of my last wishes.[11]

And so it was done. A requiem mass was conducted on November 12. Heads of state from around the world journeyed to the Cathedral of Notre Dame. The family, however, declined to attend. Philippe de

Gaulle explained that this was in keeping with the final wishes of his father.

Charles de Gaulle punctuated in death the resolution he had displayed in life. The man of destiny had always believed that he was born for some noble purpose, that his life and the history of France were intertwined. His conduct, therefore, from the earliest times served as evidence of great conviction, steadfastness in the midst of adversity, strength of character, and thus, leadership. It is no exaggeration to say that he was the embodiment of the French national spirit.

Nevertheless, de Gaulle was something of a contradiction. He dealt in absolutes, rarely acknowledging shades of gray. Authoritarian in government, he twice voluntarily relinquished great power. In his nation's weakness he found strength through intransigence. He was often cold, insensitive, and apparently unfeeling, yet his tenderness with a handicapped daughter was touching. He governed in the interest of France, refusing to see his nation relegated to the role of a bit player on the world stage.

Perhaps Charles de Gaulle asked of France more than his nation could give, to ascend to a pedestal of primacy in a world where such was neither practical nor possible. In the end, he asked no less of himself, demonstrating such personal belief in the greatness of his country and his own destiny that not even bullets on the battlefield brought fear or pause.

While his influence has given rise to a legion of admirers as well as a host of detractors, the legacy of Charles de Gaulle is one of leadership through adversity and commitment to an ideal. Such, in itself, is grandeur.

Epilogue

CHARLES DE GAULLE EXHIBITED A COMPLEX PERSONALITY THAT WAS driven by an unshakable belief in his own destiny—a destiny shaped by the hand of the Almighty and purposely interwoven with the future of France.

He rarely displayed emotion and counted few close friends. Those around him, however, acknowledged that he showed no fear. In battle, he never flinched, calm in the assurance that no bullet could kill him until his mission was complete, his destiny fulfilled.

France had always been a great nation, and during its most difficult period in modern times Charles de Gaulle emerged as its national conscience. France was foremost, and de Gaulle was her sacred defender. Intransigence was his diplomatic weapon of choice, and often the only weapon at his disposal.

During World War II, the French leader was approached by Clementine Churchill, the wife of British prime minister Winston Churchill, who remarked that it would be wise not to hate the allies of France more than the nation's enemies. He replied that France had no friends, only interests.

In truth, de Gaulle might have made the same comment about himself. De Gaulle knew the nature of hollow friendship, promises broken. He had seen the honor of France sullied by its regrettable policy of appeasement of the Nazis and the sell-out of Czechoslovakia prior to the outbreak of war in 1939. He had personally suffered, perhaps more than most, as Marshal Pétain and the collaborationist Vichyites consented to the humiliating treaty of June 1940.

The restoration of France as a player in European affairs and on the world stage required a personality such as de Gaulle. Otherwise, a defeated nation would have been relegated to the role of bit player—either occupied by the Nazis or dominated by the superpowers and supplanted once and for all by the preeminence of Great Britain in Western Europe. In response to the challenge, de Gaulle exhibited the force of personality and strength of character which maintained, to the highest possible degree, the independence of France during a period of the nation's greatest dependence on other governments. After all, the interests of Great Britain and the United States were, by definition, self-serving. Logically, the interests of France should be the same.

De Gaulle saw himself as keeper and custodian of his country's honor, and, therefore, its future. That future would be uniquely French, free from the onerous diktat of a sworn enemy or from being swept along with the tide of political affairs which served the interests of other nations. The leadership lessons derived from de Gaulle's conduct are relevant today. In fact, they are timeless. Confidence tinged with arrogance inspired a people. Conviction that his was a higher purpose, transcending the mundane, base or shallow, offered a vision. A willingness to risk his own life and the lives of his family conveyed extraordinary commitment.

During his lifetime, a cult of personality developed around de Gaulle, assigning to him attributes of courage, fortitude, and political acumen almost larger than life. While there may have been exaggerations, his conduct was proof enough that the spark of greatness was within him. He lived an austere life, never seeking personal wealth or allowing the distractions of ease to interfere with his higher calling. Uncompromising, sometimes rude, contentious and ungrateful, he proved that leadership is not a function of good humor or affability. The masses will follow a leader who does the right thing, demonstrating conviction and perseverance, and wielding power that is understood to be for the public good.

De Gaulle embodied each of these traits. A remarkable man presented with remarkable circumstances during a global tumult that is not likely to be repeated, he led France with calm resolve, apologized to no one for his love of his country and its people, and forged a lasting place in the nation's history. He did not seek to be loved or even validated, confident that time would reveal that his judgment and deeds were correct.

The paradox of de Gaulle, which elevates his leadership style from the ordinary to the transcendent, lies with the man's complexity. In arrogance and with soaring ego, he gave all to France and was, therefore, selfless. In aloofness and intransigence, he was immovable, yet transformed his country from a defeated and destitute nation to one of remarkable influence in the modern era. Throughout history, it may be said of a relative few that their influence shaped the course of events quite nearly as much as the converse. In life he was a firebrand whose restless nature ultimately fostered stability, in death a national hero whose own funerary instructions were virtually devoid of pomp and circumstance. However, in eschewing posthumous accolades or flowery eulogies, he skillfully merged his own life with that of France. The resurgent nation was, in itself, his lasting memorial.

Four decades after their term at the École Supérieure, General André Laffargue remembered de Gaulle. "He walked very straight, stiff and solemn, strutting as though he were moving his own statue. His face struck me and I could not help saying to myself, 'Well, there is someone who thinks no small beer of himself!' The two years that I spent with Charles de Gaulle at the Ecole de Guerre did away with this first unfavorable impression and made me ashamed of having had it."[1]

Of course, it must be considered that these words were written during the 1960s, when de Gaulle had achieved near mythical status. Laffargue had actually opposed de Gaulle during the Vichy years and even testified on behalf of Marshal Pétain during his post–World War II trial for treason. De Gaulle's power and influence compelled at least some one-time adversaries to reconsider their positions.

Others remained ardent opponents, but in the end their perspective mattered little. The prime mover in the life of Charles de Gaulle was the elevation of the greatness of France among nations. In this endeavor, there can be little dispute that he was successful.

Notes

PROLOGUE

1. Wernick et al., *Blitzkrieg*, p. 120.
2. "General De Gaulle," *TAC News*, p. 2.
3. Ibid.

Chapter 1: Child of Flanders

1. Cook, *Charles de Gaulle,* p. 28.
2. Ledwidge, *De Gaulle,* p. 4.
3. Schoenbrun, *The Three Lives of Charles de Gaulle,* p. 17.
4. Ibid., p. 22.
5. Lacouture, *De Gaulle,* p. 3.
6. Ibid., p. 13.
7. Ibid., pp. 9–10.
8. Ibid., p. 13.
9. Schoenbrun, pp. 23–25.
10. Cook, p. 26.
11. Ibid., introduction.

Chapter 2: Crucible of War

1. Lacouture, *De Gaulle,* p.18.
2. Cook, *Charles de Gaulle,* p. 28.
3. Lacouture, p. 19.
4. Ibid., pp. 19–21.
5. Schoenbrun, *The Three Lives of Charles de Gaulle,* pp. 26–27.

6. Crozier, *De Gaulle*, p. 29.
7. Cook, p. 29.
8. Lacouture, p. 23.
9. Cook, p. 29.
10. Ibid., p. 30
11. Lacouture, p. 25.
12. Ibid., pp. 29–31.
13. Cook, p. 29.
14. Lacouture, p. 28.
15. Werth, *De Gaulle*, p. 71.
16. Lacouture, p. 29.
17. Ibid.
18. Ibid., p. 30.
19. Ibid.
20. Ibid., p. 31.
21. Cook, p. 30.
22. Lacouture, p. 31.
23. Schoenbrun, p. 29.
24. Ibid., p. 30.
25. Lacouture, pp. 38–39.
26. Cook, p. 31.
27. Lacouture, p. 38.
28. Ibid., pp. 48–49.
29. Ibid., p. 45.
30. Ledwidge, *De Gaulle*, p. 24.
31. Lacouture, p. 49.
32. Ibid., p. 53.
33. Crawley, *De Gaulle*, p. 32.
34. Schoenbrun, p. 37.

Chapter 3: The Young Lion

1. Ledwidge, *De Gaulle*, p. 26.
2. Lacouture, *De Gaulle*, p. 57.
3. Ibid., p. 57.
4. Ibid.
5. Schoenbrun, *The Three Lives of Charles de Gaulle*, p. 38.
6. Lacouture, p. 59.
7. Ibid., p. 60.
8. Ibid, p. 61.
9. Schoenbrun, p. 41.
10. Cook, *Charles de Gaulle*, p. 34.

11. Lacouture, p. 64.
12. Ledwidge, p. 29.
13. Lacouture, p. 60.
14. Crawley, *De Gaulle*, p. 45.
15. Cook, p. 36.
16. Ibid., p. 37.
17. Ibid., p. 38.

Chapter 4: Restless Recalcitrant

1. Lacouture, *De Gaulle,* p. 78.
2. Ibid., p. 79.
3. Cook, *Charles de Gaulle*, p. 47.
4. Ibid., p. 42.
5. Ibid., p. 43.
6. Lacouture, p. 101.
7. Cook, p. 43.
8. Ibid., p. 45.
9. Crozier, *De Gaulle*, p. 52.
10. Ibid., p. 85.
11. Cook, p. 46.
12. Ibid., p. 47.
13. Ibid.
14. Masson, *De Gaulle*, p. 18.
15. Lacouture, p. 131.
16. Masson, pp. 15–20.
17. Lacouture, p. 139.
18. Ibid., p. 141.
19. Ibid., p. 151.
20. Ibid., p. 159.
21. Ibid., pp. 160–65.
22. Cook, p. 52.

Chapter 5: Soul of France

1. Lacouture, *De Gaulle*, p. 154.
2. Werth, *De Gaulle*, p. 85.
3. Crawley, *De Gaulle*, p. 94.
4. Masson, *De Gaulle*, pp. 25–26.
5. Cook, *Charles de Gaulle*, p. 54.
6. Lacouture, p. 179.
7. Crawley, pp. 99–100.

8. Lacouture, p. 184.
9. Ibid., p. 185.
10. Cook, p. 61.
11. Ledwidge, *De Gaulle*, p. 54.
12. Shirer, *The Collapse of the Third Republic*, pp. 761–62.
13. Crawley, p. 104.
14. Cook, p. 64.
15. Ibid.
16. Lacouture, p. 197.
17. Churchill, *The Gathering Storm*, p. 198.
18. Lacouture, p. 199.
19. Ibid., p. 200.
20. Ibid., pp. 200–201.
21. Ibid., p. 201.
22. Williams, *The Last Great Frenchman*, pp. 101–4.
23. Cook, p. 72.
24. Ibid., p. 72.

Chapter 6: Out of Ashes

1. Schoenbrun, *The Three Lives of Charles de Gaulle*, p. 84.
2. Cook, *Charles de Gaulle*, p. 74.
3. Ibid.
4. Shirer, *The Collapse of the Third Republic*, p. 862.
5. Ibid., p. 880.
6. Cook, pp. 76–79.
7. Lacouture, pp. 236–37.
8. Ibid., pp. 242–43.
9. Cook, pp. 85–87.
10. Ibid., pp. 120–23.
11. Ledwidge, *De Gaulle*, p. 89.
12. Cook, p. 125.
13. Lacouture, p. 288.
14. Cook, pp. 163–64.
15. Lacouture, p. 398.
16. Ibid., p. 399.
17. Cook, p. 187.
18. Ledwidge, pp. 142–47.
19. Lacouture, p. 445.
20. Ibid., p. 521.
21. Ibid., pp. 525–26.

Chapter 7: Triumphant Return

1. Ledwidge, *De Gaulle*, p. 172.
2. Cook, *Charles de Gaulle*, p. 228.
3. Eisenhower, *Crusade in Europe*, p. 296.
4. Cook, p. 245.
5. Lacouture, *De Gaulle*, p. 578.
6. Cook, p. 190.
7. Ledwidge, p. 208.

Chapter 8: Vive la France

1. Lacouture, *De Gaulle*, p. 130.
2. Cook, *Charles De Gaulle*, p. 301.
3. Williams, *The Last Great Frenchman,* p. 318.
4. Cook, p. 305.
5. Williams, p. 336.
6. Cook, p. 319.
7. Ibid., p. 334.
8. Jackson, *Charles de Gaulle*, pp. 102–8.
9. Cook, pp. 405–6.
10. Jackson, pp. 128–29.
11. Lacouture, pp. 593–94.

Epilogue

1. Crawley, *De Gaulle*, p. 67.

Select Bibliography

Churchill, Winston. *The Gathering Storm*. Vol. 1 of *The Second World War*. Boston: Houghton Mifflin Company, 1948.

Cook, Don. *Charles de Gaulle: A Biography*. New York: Putnam Publishing Group, 1983.

Crawley, Aidan. *De Gaulle*. New York: The Bobbs-Merrill Company, Inc., 1969.

Crozier, Brian. *De Gaulle: The First Complete Biography*. New York: Charles Scribner's Sons, 1973.

de Gaulle, Charles. *Memoirs of Hope: Renewal and Endeavor*. New York: Simon and Schuster, 1971.

Eisenhower, Dwight D. *Crusade in Europe*. Garden City, NY: Doubleday & Company, Inc., 1948.

"General De Gaulle: Vers l'Armée de Métier." *TAC News* (July–August 2003): 2.

Huddleston, Sisley. *France: The Tragic Years, 1939–1947*. New York: Devlin-Adair Company, 1965.

Jackson, Julian. *Charles de Gaulle*. London: Haus Publishing, 2004.

Lacouture, Jean. *De Gaulle: The Rebel, 1890–1944*. New York: W. W. Norton & Company, 1990.

———. *De Gaulle: The Ruler, 1945–1970*. New York: W. W. Norton & Company, 1992.

Ledwidge, Bernard. *De Gaulle*. New York: St. Martin's Press, 1982.

Luethy, Herbert. *France against Herself*. New York: Meridian Books, 1960.

Masson, Phillipe. *De Gaulle*. New York: Ballantine Books, 1972.

Mauriac, Claude. *The Other de Gaulle, 1944–1954*. New York: John Day Company, 1970.

Schoenbrun, David. *The Three Lives of Charles de Gaulle: A Biography*. New York: Atheneum, 1966.

Shirer, William L. *The Collapse of the Third Republic.* New York: Simon and Schuster, 1969.

Viorst, Milton. *Hostile Allies: FDR and Charles de Gaulle.* New York: The Macmillan Company, 1965.

Wernick, Robert, and the editors of Time–Life Books. *Blitzkrieg.* World War II series. New York: Time-Life Books, 1976.

Werth, Alexander. *De Gaulle: A Political Biography.* New York: Simon and Schuster, 1965.

Williams, Charles. *The Last Great Frenchman: A Life of General de Gaulle.* New York: John Wiley & Sons, Inc. 1993.

Index